QuickBooks:

The 2016 QuickBooks Complete Beginner's Guide — Learn Everything You Need To Know To Keep Your Books

Ralph McKinnon

Ralph McKinnon

© Copyright 2016 - All rights reserved.

In no way is it legal to reproduce, duplicate, or transmit any part of this document in either electronic means or in printed format. Recording of this publication is strictly prohibited and any storage of this document is not allowed unless with written permission from the publisher. All rights reserved.

The information provided herein is stated to be truthful and consistent, in that any liability, in terms of inattention or otherwise, by any usage or abuse of any policies, processes, or directions contained within is the solitary and utter responsibility of the recipient reader. Under no circumstances will any legal responsibility or blame be held against the publisher for any reparation, damages, or monetary loss due to the information herein, either directly or indirectly. Respective authors own all copyrights not held by the publisher.

Legal Notice:

This book is copyright protected. This is only for personal use. You cannot amend, distribute, sell, use, quote or paraphrase any part or the content within this book without the consent of the author or copyright owner. Legal action will be pursued if this is breached.

Disclaimer Notice:

Please note the information contained within this document is for educational and entertainment purposes only. Every attempt has been made to provide accurate, up to date and reliable complete information. No warranties of any kind are expressed or implied. Readers acknowledge that the author is not engaging in the rendering of legal, financial, medical or professional advice.

By reading this document, the reader agrees that under no circumstances are we responsible for any losses, direct or indirect, which are incurred as a result of the use of information contained within this document, including, but not limited to, —errors, omissions, or inaccuracies.

Table Of Contents

Introduction 9
Chapter 1 Getting Started 13
   Steps For Getting Started With QuickBooks 13
   Advantages of using QuickBooks 19
   Starting a new company file 22
   Managing payment methods 23
Chapter 2 Recording Transactions 27
   Record Register Transactions in QuickBooks 27
   Create a New Budget with QuickBooks 30
   Setting up a Customer List in QuickBooks 32
   Organizing your accounts receivable 34
   Record sales and payments 35
Chapter 3 QuickBooks Tools 39
   Accountant Tool Box: 39
   Accountant Center: 41
   Batch Enter Transactions: 41
   Client Data Review: 42
   Send Portable Company File: 42
   Enhanced Report Layout: 43
   Field Search Boxes on Customize: 43
   Annotate Reports with Comments: 43
   Send Multiple Reports in a Single Email: 44
   QuickBooks Statement Writer 47

Ralph McKinnon

Chapter 4 Keeping Your Financial Records Tidy 57
   Resolve your QuickBooks bank accounts regularly 57
   Keep updating loan account balances 58
   Check for any orphan payments 58
   Review your balance sheet regularly 59
   Tips for dealing with deposits in QuickBooks 59
   Financial Tips for Business Owners 61

Chapter 5 Basic Troubleshooting 71
   Update the data file failures: 72
   When rebuilding of the data file fails: 72
   You have lost connection to the data file: 73
   The reinstall fails: 74
   When on multiuser mode they are slow: 74
   The client machine on QuickBooks isn't able to locate a data file on the server: 75
   Unable to find the licensing information: 75
   A new printer will not print: 76
   You've lost the admin password: 76
   You aren't able to copy or even move the QuickBooks data file: 76

Chapter 6 Ten Common Mistakes To Avoid When Using QuickBooks 79
   Getting Started: 79

Chapter 7 Recording Transactions In QuickBooks 123
   How to Record Transactions in QuickBooks? 123

Chapter 8 Setting Up Bank Accounts And Credit Cards Through QuickBooks 137

Chapter 9 Guide To The Interface Of QuickBooks 145
Chapter 10 How To Navigate Through QuickBooks.........155
Chapter 11 Advanced Tips And Shortcuts For QuickBooks Users... 159
Conclusion...197

Ralph McKinnon

Introduction

I want to thank you for selecting and purchasing this book – "QuickBooks: The 2016 QuickBooks Complete Beginner's Guide – Learn Everything You Need To Know To Keep Your Books." As you may know, QuickBooks is an accounting and bookkeeping software package that is developed by Intuit. This application has managed to bring together the various processes and tasks of accounting into a single easy-to-use system.

QuickBooks has been created mainly for businesses and organizations that are small to medium in size. This software provides accounting applications not only on the premises but also on the cloud. The primary function of QuickBooks is to simplify the accounting tasks which often involve working on multiple spreadsheets, tracking sheets and tables. All of these things are essential for recording as well as maintaining the various accounting functions which are carried out daily in any business. This application even takes taxation into consideration as accounting figures can be reconciled easily. Another great aspect of this software is that it can be customized as per the requirements of your business operations so that you can use it better.

Have you just started using QuickBooks and found it rather scary? Maybe you heard about this software and wanted to know more about it? Well, whatever the reason, you don't have to worry anymore. After all, you have just chosen this book. This book will help you learn everything about QuickBooks and how it can assist in maintaining the finances and records of your organization.

Do you want to know something awesome? QuickBooks can do more than just keep a register of the daily business transactions. It can even help you keep track of your finances, your payments, your receipts, and even your customers!

All you need to keep running your business smoothly can be found in QuickBooks. In the same way, everything you need to know to start using QuickBooks in your business has its place in this book. Here, you will be learning how to get started with QuickBooks, keeping a track of your incomes and sales, managing your customer lists, maintaining your invoices, receipts, and payments among many other things.

The main function of this software is to minimize having to work on multiple tables, spreadsheets, and tracking sheets that are important for recording and maintaining different accounting tasks carried on in a business on a daily basis. For the purpose of taxation, accounting figures can be easily reconciled by making use of QuickBooks. Intuit developed this software and it provides the option of customization according to the needs of your business operations by making use of this software.

Are you just getting started with QuickBooks? Does it seem a little scary? Well, don't worry. In this book you will learn everything there is to know about QuickBooks to help you in maintaining your business records and finances. QuickBooks isn't just about maintaining a record of day-to-day business transactions, but it also helps you in keeping track of your customers, your finances, your payments, and your receipts.

Everything related to running a business finds its place in this software. In this book you will learn about everything from getting started with QuickBooks, maintaining your customer lists, keeping track of your sales and incomes,

Ralph McKinnon

managing your invoices, managing your receipts and payments, and more.

So, without further ado, let us get started! Happy Reading!

Chapter 1
Getting Started

Steps For Getting Started With QuickBooks

QuickBooks is the one-stop accounting solution for all business owners. It's an online accounting software and it offers a variety of financial tools that range from recording invoices, transactions, and account tracking to managing customer lists, payment options, and even your bank accounts. This is a very useful tool and it is user friendly, but it might seem confusing and even slightly overwhelming in the beginning. In this chapter we will deal with the process of getting started with QuickBooks.

Consult your accountant:

The first thing you might want to do is consult your accountant before you migrate your finances to QuickBooks. You can make use of ProAdvisor, an online accountant service provided by Intuit. Most of the accountants would support this service, so you could also consult with a local accountant. By doing so, you can obtain information regarding the specifics of your business that QuickBooks would need, like your business structure, the appropriate conventions for tracking your expenses, and the legal local or state compliances you will have to follow.

Familiarize yourself with the software:

This is very important. However comfortable you are with numbers, you will need to spend some time exploring the "Getting Started" tab included in the tutorials. This will provide you with the introduction to QuickBooks features like managing your bills, sending and receiving invoices, and so on. Revenue is classified as "Money In" and "Money Out" signifies expenses. Money flow is mapped through your business in a chart referred to as "Getting Around."

Setting up a secure environment:

When there is money at stake, security is of utmost importance, especially when all your financial information is stored in one place. Before you start entering all your financial information, go to "Your Account" tab and change your password. Set a password that is complex and unique; also change it once every quarter. You should also keep changing the passwords QuickBooks stores, along with your online banking IDs in your bank's website, as well as QuickBooks.

Enter your business details:

Now that you are acquainted with the basics of QuickBooks and setting passwords, go to "Preferences" under the "Company" tab and enter the financial details of your company. The important items you need to enter are the business structure, reporting forms, Tax ID and the reporting calendar. But the details can differ from one company to other. You should double-check all the details with your accountant or financial advisor.

Entering customer information:

Now, proceed to the "Customer" tab and start entering your client's information. Name, address, and email are the important details you need to fill out, but don't forget about the "Payment Method" option, because this is very critical.

Before filling out this option, crosscheck the method of payment your customers would prefer and set this information accordingly. If possible, it would be better if you can generate a trial invoice for your clients. Confirm with them if the details are as they should be.

Syncing your bank account:

One frequent question asked by most QuickBooks users is how to add their bank account to their QuickBooks. It is an extremely simple process to sync your bank accounts to the company file. You will need to open the option Chart of Accounts. Proceed to the option "Add New Account" and select "Bank" as the account type. Now you just need to enter your bank information. The same steps can also be used to sync your credit cards, loans, and your equity.

Enter the basic vendor and employee information:

Go to the "Vendors" and "Employees" tab. Start by filling out their contact information of the employees who work for you and the vendors who sell to you. You have the option of not entering all the information QuickBooks prompts you to enter. The "report" button on the right side of the screen will help you verify the information entered by you.

Start tracking the flow of money:

This is slightly tricky: you will need to account the actual money your business has generated and the amount that goes towards expenses. Open the "Banking" tab and look at the basic reporting options that are available for tracking the money you make and the incurred expenses. You can connect all your financial accounts like your bank accounts, credit cards, and so on from here. Make sure you can write checks using the option "Write Checks" and you can handle your sales and costs with the "Cash Expense," "Credit Card Expense," and "Deposit" tabs. Do trial runs with all these options to make sure you understand them correctly and also to check if QuickBooks is correctly recording your data. You will also want to monitor all the activity going on in your account. For this purpose, go to the "Manage Users" option in Your Account to add users. Preferably, just you and your accountant make use of the Activity reports to know who and what activity has been going on in the account.

Review the expenses label:

You will need to make sure your business funds are well organized acceding to categories for tax and other regulatory purposes. Therefore, it is important that you know your business expenses. Ensure you know how to track your cash expenses by hand and also the automatically downloaded expenses data generated by your bank or a credit card. This can be found in the "Download Transactions" option. Entering cash expenses into QuickBooks manually is a simple procedure. You just need to enter the amount corresponding to the vendor and add a memo to it. All the expense data generated by your bank or credit cards can be automatically uploaded to this. Confirm with your accountant whether or not the data being entered is correct.

Create your first profit and loss report:

After reviewing all your expense labels, it is time for you to determine the profit your business has generated. There are full sets of reporting tools Intuit has made available. For now, go to the Profit & Loss option within the Report tab. This function, like its name suggests, will add up all the income that was generated and deduct all the expenses that were incurred for a given period of time in QuickBooks. Among other things, this option will help you determine the amount of tax you are liable to pay on your potential profit. You can capture your financial statements as well as all the other reports you deem necessary and run them by your accountant from time to time by making use of the "Memorize" function of QuickBooks.

Once you have understood the basics of QuickBooks like generating invoices, adding bank accounts, sales tracking, monitoring your expenses, and determining your profit and loss, you can move onto adding other features you want. There are QuickBooks mobile apps that will let you carry on with your transactions while you are working remotely or on vacation.

Advantages of using QuickBooks

Regardless of the nature of the business you are involved in, keeping an accurate set of books of accounts will always come in handy. Without having accurate business records, it will get difficult for you to attract the required funding. Business records are the first documents given to potential investors and lenders. Also, it gets difficult to file your taxes if your books are unorganized. It can also land you in trouble with the IRS. Here are all the different advantages QuickBooks provides its users:

Ease of use:

One problem most of the accounting programs pose is that they are difficult to use and are often cumbersome. QuickBooks is designed to be user friendly and easy to understand, even for all those business owners who don't have any accounting or commerce background.

Integration:

QuickBooks is capable of being integrated with different programs. Once they have filled in all their business related transactions and information in QuickBooks, they can easily export this information to other apps, such as a taxation app for calculating the tax payable. This program can also be integrated with Microsoft Excel, which makes it easy to import your data from other sources to QuickBooks.

Customization:

There are different ready-to-use templates provided by QuickBooks that business owners can make use of while creating their invoices, spreadsheets, business charts, and plans. You can also customize the look and feel of all the documents. It is incredibly helpful that invoices can also be customized because this lets business owners add logos but they can also add information about each line item included in there. This makes it really easy for the customers for reconciling their invoices and for making timely payments.

Check signing:

If you are in the habit of writing a lot of checks for your business, making use of QuickBooks can help you save a lot of time. QuickBooks allows business owners to scan and upload their signatures. These signatures can then be used to prepare checks for business transactions. This is much simpler than writing out all the checks manually.

Starting a new company file

When you start a new company file on QuickBooks it lets you create present charts of the accounts based on your type of business. You can customize these charts of accounts by adding, modifying, or deleting the accounts according to your needs. For creating a new company file that has blank charts of accounts, you will have to select the options that will help in reducing the number of accounts created by QuickBooks. QuickBooks will still create new charts of accounts when you are creating a new company file, but the number of accounts in it will be restricted and you have the option of either deleting or marking these accounts as inactive. Open your QuickBooks and choose the "File" tab and select the option "New Company." Click on the option "Express Start." Now, you have to create the new company file. To create the file, you will have to enter information about your business like the Company Name. When entering the Industry for your business you can click the option "Help Me Choose" for finding the right Industry if needed. If not, you can select the "Other" or "None" option. After entering the Company Type you have to enter the Tax ID Number. Once you have filled out the entire information click on "Continue" to proceed further. Fill in your business contact details and select the option "Create Company File." Click on "Start Working" after this and choose the tab "Lists" and select the option "Chart of Accounts." Your Chart of Accounts will have only five accounts mentioned in it. If you don't make use of payroll, then mark this account as inactive. You have the option of deleting accounts you don't make use of, but it is advisable that you don't do so.

Managing payment methods

A frequently asked question regards the manner users can manage methods of payments. It is really easy to set up the initial credit card and debit card details in the "Receipt Bank" under the list of methods of payments, but it isn't that simple to manage payments made by cash, check, or any other method not connected to a credit card.

Cash:

It would be useful if you could set up one of the payment methods as "Cash." This way, this option can be used for all future transactions made by the company from its cash fund. It all depends upon the manner in which you want to manage your books, but a majority of the QuickBooks users often create a petty cash account with their QuickBooks for keeping an eye on the cash assets of their company. For all the cash receipts or payments requiring reimbursement you can create a separate cash payment method with the "Receipt Bank as Cash to be Reimbursed" or any other name you want. You can then link this particular account with any other account in your QuickBooks from which the reimbursement will eventually be made. Usually, cash receipts don't come with a credit card number that can be fed into the system, and the system on its own will not make an assumption that the payment was in cash. This is when you can consider making use of the supplier rules for your benefit. Also, you get to select the default method of payment for a user according to a by-user basis so the system would automatically record any transaction as a cash transaction if it doesn't have a credit or a debit card number.

Checks:

Checks should be dealt with similarly to cash. It is advisable you don't enter the check number on the items and don't make use of the check number for referencing an entry in the Receipt Bank, as this would just confuse the system. For instance, QuickBooks can mistake a check that ends with 4389 as a credit card ending in 4389. Instead, it would be better if you treat checks as you would treat cash. Have a standard payment method by check that can be manually assigned to the items linked to your checking account.

Credit cards:

Most financial institutions will treat credit cards as a separate account that can be linked directly to QuickBooks. However, all institutions don't provide this function. If you just want to track your credit card as another monthly expense to be paid, then this is the section for you. If you want, you have the option of treating credit cards the same way you treat your checking and other bank accounts on QuickBooks. If your bank doesn't provide an online feed for credit cards, then you can link this to your Receipt Bank. In this way, it's linked to your bank account in the same fashion as your bills. This will help you properly reconcile your accounts and allow you to keep track of your credit card expenses.

PayPal:

If you are maintaining your PayPal account as a bank account in your QuickBooks, then you can make use of this to pay for transactions in Receipt Bank.

Direct Debit:

When you pay some bills by direct debit in your account, then you can treat direct debit as a payment indication. The best option is to set up direct debit as a method of payment within the Receipt Bank, and then you can link this to your bank account in QuickBooks so your bills can be paid directly out of this bank. You can then set all the supplier rules for allowing direct debit as a method of payment for various bills as well as invoices from suppliers that would be directly debited from your account.

Chapter 2
Recording Transactions

Record Register Transactions in QuickBooks

By making use of the "Register Window," you can record checks, deposits, and various account transfers in QuickBooks. The "Register Window" resembles an ordinary paper register you would use for keeping track of all your transactions, like your bank account. QuickBooks allows you to directly enter transactions into the account register. For entering a bank account transaction, directly go into the account register and follow the simple steps given in this section.

For opening the Account Register, choose the Banking tab and click on the "Use Register" option. At times when you follow this procedure, QuickBooks will open the "Use Register" dialog box and will ask you to select the particular bank account you want to be displayed in the register. For selecting the account, you would want to use, open the "Select Account" list, and then select the bank account you want and click okay. Then, the Register window will open. If QuickBooks shows the register of a particular account other than the one you would want to use, select "Banking" and choose the option "Use Register" once more. Now, the "Use Register" dialog box must open.

For recording the date of a particular deposit, payment, or transfer, make use of the date column given in the register. You can enter the date in the mm/dd/yyyy format. You can also click on the calendar button toward the right of the date field so the calendar shows and you can select the date from the calendar. Now, you will have to assign a transaction number, but this is entirely optional. You can make use of the number column for uniquely identifying the transaction. If it is for checks, then you can record the check number in this field. For transfers and deposits, you don't necessarily have to record a transaction number.

Make use of the payee field for recording the payee for a particular check, the customer who is making a deposit, or some other particular information in case of a transfer. For selecting an existing customer, vendor, or the name from one of the QuickBooks lists, just click on the arrow present on the field payee. When you do this, QuickBooks automatically displays the list of recorded names. You just need to click one of the names from the list and provide the transaction amount. Make use of the payment column if you have to describe a transaction made by check or for a transfer moving money from one account to another.

Make use of the deposit column if you have to describe a deposit or transfer made to the account. For transactions made by check you will have to identify the account along with the expense aligned with the particular check. For a deposit, you can make use of the account field for identifying the corresponding sales revenue account linked to such a deposit. For any transfer transaction, you will have to make use of the account field for identifying the bank account involved. You can enter the name of the account in the account box or you can open the drop down list of accounts and choose a particular account you want by clicking on it.

If you want, you can provide a memo description by making use of the "Memo" field by providing a brief description of the payment, deposit, or transfer transaction. You can split the transaction if you desire. This means you can assign the same transaction to more than one account by selecting the "Split" option. In the register window, this transaction would be displayed in the "Split" area. The "Split" area lets you split a particular transaction among several accounts. For instance, a check to pay for office supplies as well as computer expenses can be split between two accounts. In a similar manner, a deposit made to account for two revenue items can also be split. Once you are done splitting the transaction, you will need to click on the "Close" option. For recording a transaction into the register, you just need to click on the "Record" option and QuickBooks calculates the account balance and adjusts the ending balance according to the new transaction.

Create a New Budget with QuickBooks

Once you have a budget, you will need to record the same in the QuickBooks. For doing so, just follow the simple steps mentioned in this section. Select the option "Company" and click on the "Planning and Budgeting" option. From this, click on the "Set up Budgets" command. Now, QuickBooks displays the "Create a New Budget" window; make use of this window by recording the expected amount of revenue and the expense account for a single month during the year for which you are doing the budgeting. Click on the "Create a New Budget" button. This would open up the "Create New Budget" dialog box that you would make use of for creating a new budget.

Select the fiscal year for which you are making the budget. Depending upon the year for which you want to create a budget, choose that option from the list. Depending upon the type of budget you want to create, you can either select the "Profit & Loss" or the "Balance Sheet" button. If it is the "Profit and Loss" budget, then click "Next" and if it is the "Balance Sheet" budget, then click "Finish" to complete the budget. You need to understand that different approaches should be adopted depending upon the kind of budget you want to make. For a profit and loss budget, only the expected revenue or expenses will be taken into consideration. But for a balance sheet budget, you will have to take into consideration the ending balances of different accounts such as equity, assets, and liability at the end of every month. You will have to specify any additional profit or loss criteria you would like to include in your budget and once you do this, click "Next." You can select the option of creating a budget right from scratch or from any previous information previously stored. Depending upon what you want, you can select the option "Create Budget From

Scratch" or "Create Budget From Previous Year's Data." When you are done, just click "Finish" and QuickBooks will display the "Set Up Budgets" window.

Setting up a Customer List in QuickBooks

A "Customer's List," like the name suggests, will help you keep track of all your customers and their information. For instance, this list will help you keep track of the shipping and billing addresses of your customers on the list. Here are the steps you will have to follow for adding a customer to this list.

The first step is for you to select the "Lists" tab and click on the "Customer Job List" option. QuickBooks will then open up the "Customer Job List" window. This window provides you with the option of editing customer information; you can delete customers, print the list, and so on. For adding a new customer to this, click on the "Customer Job" option and click on the "New" option. This would make QuickBooks display the "New Customer" window. Make use of the "Customer Name" box for giving the particular customer a short name. You needn't enter the full name of the customer in this box, because all these details directly go into the "Company Name" box. You just need to have an abbreviated form of your customer's name so it is easy to refer to such a customer throughout the accounting process within QuickBooks. Ignore the "Opening Balance" and the related boxes. If you make an entry in these boxes, then you will have to make corrections to incomplete bookkeeping. In the "Address Info" tab, fill out the billing and shipping address, the name of the company, contact name and number, fax number, and so on. You can always add additional information about the customer, and for doing this you can make use of the "Type" drop-down list box for categorizing a particular customer into a customer type. Make use of the "Terms" drop-down list for identifying customers who have made a default payment method. For a default in their sales rep make use of the red drop-down list and for the default method for sending invoices you can make use of the "Preferred Send Method." You can add as many additional fields as you want to according to your convenience. Select the "Payment Info" tab and record the customer's account number, credit limit, and preferred method of payment. The "Job Info" tab is optional and you can make use of this tab for describing the kind of job being performed for a particular customer.

Organizing your accounts receivable

This will help you to automatically manage invoicing and tracking as well as reporting, regardless of time and place. Do you provide goods or perhaps render services before you get an actual payment? The money owed to you is referred to as accounts receivable. It means there is income due to you but that you are waiting to receive it.

It is important to manage your accounts receivable because it will help you maintain a healthy cash flow, make sure you are being paid, flag any late payments, send reminders for any overdue payments, and automatically record payments. This will help you keep track of who owes money to whom. Every invoice created in QuickBooks is put in accounts receivable and when the invoice has been paid, this is recorded in the customer's account. All this information will be available to you in just a click. You can access this information anytime, from anywhere, as long as you have a device that is compatible with QuickBooks and you have a working Internet connection. All the accounts receivable data, like the amount a customer owes you, frequency of a payment, any delay in payment, etc., will be available to you because QuickBooks syncs all this instantly to your phone or your laptop.

Record sales and payments

In this section you will learn the manner in which you can record your sales and payments in QuickBooks.

The first step is to record the sales with a Sales Receipt. If you sell something and you immediately get paid for it, then record this with a sales receipt. In the Navigation Bar that's under the Transactions tab, click on the option "Sales." Now, go to "New Transactions" and click on the option "Sales Receipt." Enter all the required customer information here and then save it. For recording sales with an invoice, you will have to click the "Plus Sign Menu" and then under the Customers option, click on "Invoice." Enter all the required customer information and then save it. Whenever you receive payment from your customer, record the same in "Receive Payments" by clicking the plus sign and under Customers you need to select the option "Received Payment." You will need to enter their method of payment and then save it. For recording deposits, again click on the plus sign and select "Other" and "Bank Deposit." Select the proper account and then select either "Existing Payment" or "New Deposit." Then, save the changes you have made. For keeping track of any pending invoices from customers, like billable hours or any purchased goods, go to the Navigation Bar and select the option "Customers." Click on the link "Unbilled Activity" and in the color-coded bar you can see if any change has been made. For reminding yourself that you need to invoice your customers, go to the "Plus" menu again and under the option "Customers" select "Delayed Charge." Select a particular customer and enter the product or service that requires an invoice. Keep a weekly timesheet and keep adding any billable items as well as daily hours to it and save the changes made. To invoice your customers for all the billable hours, you will have to open the "Plus" menu again and under the option "Customers" you will have to select "Invoice" and add the billable hours you have recorded in the weekly timesheet. If any of your customers wants credit that can be used later or wants to apply for an invoice right now, then you can generate a credit memo for this purpose. Go to the "Plus" menu, choose a customer, and enter all their billing information and then select the corresponding goods or services and any other taxes or applicable discounts. Save the credit memo. If a particular customer wants their money back, then record the payment that has been made to them by using a Refund Receipt under the "Plus" menu under the "Customers" option.

Choose a customer and enter all their billing information and also select the corresponding goods or services and any other taxes or applicable discounts. Save the Refund Receipt. For analyzing your sales, what you have sold and to whom you have made the sales, then select the "Reports" option from the Navigation Bar.

Ralph McKinnon

Chapter 3
QuickBooks Tools

QuickBooks Accountant Desktop provides solutions for many of the ways in which accountants work with the data their clients give them. This software has been designed in such a manner that it improves the efficiency of accounting professionals and also helps in reviewing the QuickBooks data of their clients. The features described in this chapter will help you get the most from QuickBooks.

Accountant Tool Box:

With this, you can unlock the access to any of the accounting tools on the go. For accountants who are working on their client's books on site, this is really helpful. Also for business owners without any accounting background, they can generate statements and maintain accounts without much difficulty. You can work easily and efficiently with tasks required to be completed for a tax return or for making any necessary global changes. For accessing your Accountant Toolbox, while you are working on a non-accountant version of QuickBooks, you will have to ask your client to create an External Accountant user type. Then, from the menu bar, select the "Company" option, click on "Setup Users" and passwords and then follow the prompts given by QuickBooks for selecting an External Accountant user. This is required when you try to login and then unlock the Accountant Toolbox. Now, you will have to log into the non-accountant version of QuickBooks that you have with the External Accountant user name that was created for you. From the menu bar select the "Company" option, then the Accountant Toolbox and then the option of "Unlock Accountant Toolbox." When you do this you will be prompted by QuickBooks to provide your email ID as well as the password associated with your QuickBooks Accountant Desktop. This Toolbox is accessible from the company menu when you are logged in as External Accountant Access to the Accountant tools. The following tools are available in the Accountant Toolbox and they will help you to simplify the process of reviewing your clients' file.

Accountant Center:

This can be accessed from the menu bar by selecting the option of Accountant and then Accountant Center. This is also included in your Accountant Toolbox access. You can manage your tools, the banking details of your clients, access the report, and stay connected to the valuable resources. You have the option of customizing the Accountant Center according to your needs and your customized selection of all the tools as well as features will be displayed with each unique client that the QuickBooks file has managed to open. Once you have customized your Accountant Center you can open it with every client file.

Batch Enter Transactions:

This is accessible from the menu bar if you select the option "Accountant" and then "Batch Enter Transactions." If the engagement you have with your client also tends to include the entering of multiple checks, vendor bills, and customer invoices to QuickBooks, then you can make use of the "Batch Enter Transactions" window for facilitating a quick data entry.

Client Data Review:

This is accessible from the menu bar; click on "Accountant" and then on "Client Data Review." Reviewing all the files of your client can be a very time consuming process and this can help save you valuable time. With this, you can reclassify hundreds of transactions in one go. Write off open customer invoices balances in one go, fix any sales tax payments that have been incorrectly recorded, and troubleshoot any inventory issues.

Send Portable Company File:

You can access this from the menu bar by selecting "File," then "Send Company File" and within it, "Portable Company File." This option lets you create a one-click link for the exchange of files between the business owner and the clients. This is similar to the services of Dropbox that Google provides. This requires the usage of a third party shared folder that makes use of the Internet services. When you use this feature, QuickBooks automatically selects the right file. You set up a shared folder once and the same will be recorded in the settings. There won't be any need for technical support intervention from your accountant and it also eliminates frustration you might feel when trying to copy and send a file to your accountants for reviewing.

Enhanced Report Layout:

The Reports feature in QuickBooks has gotten a makeover with a fresher look. The design is modern with horizontal lines, background shading, and minimum breadth and lengthwise grid lines. Thanks to these improvements it is incredibly easy to scan an extensive report, especially when you have to view this on your computer screen.

Field Search Boxes on Customize:

This is accessible from the Modify box, which is present at the top left of the displayed report. Modifying reports has become quite easy with the added search and the alphabetically arranged data listing fields.

Annotate Reports with Comments:

This option is accessible from the Comment box that is present at the top of a report. The reports saved here have comments that can be easily accessed from the menu bar. This makes the process of interpreting reports much easier and using the comment fields helps in capturing the report content, as well as any comments you might want to communicate with the other party to whom you are addressing. These reports can be saved, printed, and emailed to your accountant or other advisor.

Send Multiple Reports in a Single Email:

This option can be accessed from the menu bar by selecting the "Reports" option and then the "Process Multiple Reports" option. There might be times when you would want to send multiple reports to your client. For doing this, all that you have to do is go to the menu bar, select "Reports" and then select "Memorized Report List." Then you can process multiple reports by going to the menu bar, selecting reports and clicking the suitable option. All these reports are simply added as multiple attachments to your email. This feature is time saving and isn't cumbersome like the earlier method.

Insights on Homepage:

This can be accessed from the tab present next to the Homepage. This provides insights on the Homepage and also offers a snapshot of your client's business and it makes it really easy for you to provide any useful recommendations to them. You can customize the information you want it to display.

Time and Expenses on Income Tracker:

This is accessible from the menu bar. Select the "Company" option and then click on "Income Tracker." For all those who want to invoice their customers for all the time spent on a particular project, do so by making use of this feature. It helps by creating a rough estimate of the time it would take for the completion of a billable project.

QuickBooks File Manager:

This is accessible from the icon that's on the desktop, either through the Accountant menu or even the Accountant Center. QuickBooks File Manager will be installed along with your accountant software. This File Manager can be used for opening and then easily managing your Client's QuickBooks files and from any particular location. You can build a client list that helps you create a virtual view of the hard drive where you store all the files, which can be stored on the hard drive as well as on the server. You will need to create user-definable client groups like Payroll Clients and

Monthly or Annual Review Clients to name a few suggestions for the manner in which you can group your clients. You will have to save file passwords of your clients in one place. The File Manager in QuickBooks will help you open the client's files without requiring the repeated input of the password. You can view critical information about your client's data without opening the file, including data in a tax form, a closing date, and so on. Client Collaborator will help you in communicating with your clients by making use of QuickBooks itself.

Send General Journal Entries:

You can send journal entries by making use of this feature. It allows you to share the changes that have been made to the client's file by making use of a very simple attachment of the journal entries of all the concerned transactions. The best manner in which you can use this feature is by having the business owner send the accountant the portable file enhanced by QuickBooks with the use of the Internet. Or you can also ask for a working copy as well as a backup. The business owners can carry on with their work in these files while the accountant can still review the files. The journal entries entered by the accountant can be directly mailed to the business owner by making use of QuickBooks, which is a very simple process. The clients will just have to click on the attachment for importing the journal entries. Isn't this simple?

Accountant's Copy:

This can be accessed from the menu bar by selecting "File" and then "Send Company File." Within this list, select the option "Accountant's Copy." This is one of the most effective ways in which you can share the access to your client's QuickBooks with your Accountant. By making use of this feature, your clients will be able to carry on with their day-to-day operations and you can review and make necessary changes to this by sitting in your own office.

QuickBooks Statement Writer

This can be accessed from the menu bar and all you will need to do is select "Accountant" or "Reports." This feature is a very powerful and flexible reporting tool that allows accountants to prepare financial statements from the data entered in QuickBooks that are in compliance with the GAAP (Generally Accepted Accounting Principles).

10 QuickBooks Reports You Should Be Using

When you are using QuickBooks, you are certain to end up relying on the Reports menu and the Report Center. However, the fact is that you will generally end up using a small number of reports. On the other hand, QuickBooks offers a rather extensive array of reports. Some of them are actually quite useful, but few people know or use them. Take a look at some reports that you should definitely try out.

Balance Sheet Previous Year Comparison:

This report can be accessed through the Company and Financial section which is present in the Reports menu. In many ways, it is just as valuable as your income statement. This report will help you compare the standings of certain balances with that of the previous year. Some of the areas which can prove to be useful are listed as follows.

- Inventory
- Accounts Receivable
- Accounts Payable
- Cash

- Other Liabilities like short term loans or lines of credit

Profit & Loss Summary Previous Year Comparison:

You can access this report through the Reports menu. Click on Company and Financial to find this report. Generally, you will end up using the Profit & Loss Summary report. However, comparing the results of the current year with that of the previous year can be rather helpful for your business. You can get a quick insight into the state of your revenue such as whether it is experiencing growth or contraction. You can also discover the rate at which your expenses are on the rise.

Statement of Cash Flows:

This report can also be accessed by means of Company and Financial. The balance reports can be used for understanding your current possessions as well as your debts. The profit and loss reports help you get a better understanding of your earnings. However, neither of these reports can help you get a clear picture of the source of your cash or where it is going. This is where the Statement of Cash Flows proves its use.

You can use it to discover more about your cash flows such as the following.

- How much cash has been earned from your sales and has been spent on the expenses.
- How the cash is flowing in or flowing out thanks to repayment, investing or borrowing activities.

In other words, you can use this report to find out the exact cause behind the increase in your bank balance or its decrease during the specified report period.

A/P Aging Summary:

It goes without saying that it is vital for you to ensure that your customers are paying you in a timely fashion. At the same time, it is incredibly important for you to make sure that your vendors are being paid by your company. After all, unpaid bills can be the cause of unnecessary emails, phone calls and other such interruptions. To help you remain on top of your dues, use the A/P Aging Summary report.

This can be found in the Reports, Vendors & Payables option. With its help, you can find out when bills are entering into the dreaded overdue status. You can get a better understanding of each amount by double clicking on each amount to open up the original transaction.

Collections Report:

As mentioned earlier, it is vital that you keep track of the collections from your customers. With QuickBooks, you will find it much easier to do so and even contact the customers who have overdue invoices. The Collections Report can be found in the Reports, Customers & Receivables section.

In the report, you will find a list of all the overdue invoices of your company along with the respective contact details of the customers. You can also use the report to send quick e-mail copies of the overdue invoices to the defaulting customers. In order to send the mail, double click on the transaction in the Collections report. You will now be viewing the invoice. Here you can also find the Send button located at the top. Click on it to open the Send invoice form. You can change the content details of the mail here from the default text given.

If you want to change the default text of the email permanently, you need to click on Edit and open the Preferences section. Click on the Send Forms option and select the Invoice option from the list title Change Default For. Here, you can make the changes and then save it by clicking OK.

Voided/Deleted Transactions Summary:

There are many reasons why you need to take a look at the transactions that have been deleted or declared void. Fraud is one of the most important reasons. Thanks to QuickBooks, it is more difficult for perpetrators to defraud you of your hard-earned money.

The Voided/Deleted Transactions Summary can be found through the Reports, Accountant & Taxes section. You can use this report to identify all the transactions that have been deleted from your QuickBooks file. You can even find out which user was responsible for deleting the transaction in the first place. As such, this tool can be rather useful even if it is not a complete solution for fraud prevention.

Trial Balance:

Many QuickBooks users tend not use this report. On the other hand, this report can be rather helpful. The Trial Balance report can be used for viewing all the account balances in a nice and concise format. You can double click on an amount in order to get more details about it. You can access the Trial Balance report through the Reports, Accountant & Taxes section.

Previous Reconciliation:

When reconciling a credit card or bank account, a good practice is to print the summary report. After all, others may end up editing a reconciled transaction by mistake causing an error in the reconciliation balance. Of course, a printed copy is helpful even though the edited transaction will still have to be sorted manually.

With Previous Reconciliation, this becomes much easier. It can be accessed through the Banking option in Reports.

Audit Trail:

Audit Trail is actually a useful report. You can use it to get the complete record of each and every entry that has been made in your QuickBooks file. On the other hand, you will certainly find a massively big report. To make it easier to search for specific records, QuickBooks has added a number of filters to it.

You can access Audit Trail through the Accountant & Taxes option from Reports. The Filters tab can be accessed by means of the Modify button on the report.

Transaction History:

The special thing about this report is that it can only be accessed in specific situations. First of all, you need to have a transaction opened up on the screen. Alternatively, you can single click on the transaction in a report. Now, you can choose the Reports section from which you can select Transaction History. With this report, you can view the entire history for that specific transaction.

Make Use of the Fixed Asset Tools

Most of the work that you will be doing in QuickBooks is short-term. However, fixed assets are a different matter altogether as you will be managing their lifecycle. Fixed assets as you already know are physical entities which are purchased for helping your business generate some revenue. Some possible fixed assets include properties and vehicles.

An asset can only be classified as a fixed asset when it has been used for more than 12 months.

You can take the help of QuickBooks to track these fixed assets certainly. On the other hand, the value of your company as well as your tax obligations will be affected by the depreciation of the book value of the fixed assets. You can work together with a third party over the life of each asset. On the other hand, you can maintain accurate records on your own with QuickBooks.

Keeping Track:

If you wish to record information on a fixed asset, the best time to do is when you are creating the transaction about its purchase. It is possible to build and item record for the fixed asset while the Item section in various forms is being filled up. You can do so for forms like Write Checks, Enter Bills, Purchase Order or Enter Credit Card Charges.

On the other hand, it is possible that you want an item record to be created for a fixed asset without processing any transaction. There are quite a few situations in which this might occur. Some of the possible situations are given below.

- Purchase of fixed assets with your personal funds
- Transfer of personal assets to the company

- Cash purchases
- Multi-item purchases

When you want to create a fixed asset item record in these situations, you need to first open the Lists menu. There, you can open the Fixed Asset Item List. In order to add a new item here, right click in the list section of the screen. From the menu, select the new option. You will notice that the New Item window is the same as what appears on the previous screen.

The Type should already have been selected as Fixed Asset. For the Asset name or number field, make sure that you enter a name that is easy for you to recognize. You should be able to identify it quickly in reports. Make sure that the right Asset Account has also been selected and then place a proper description. Don't forget to add all the other relevant details such as cost, purchase date, and so on.

As for the Sales Information fields, you do not need to do anything on them. They will only be used if and when you are selling the asset.

Fixed assets are crucial to your company and its finances. That makes them critical to your use of QuickBooks.

Chapter 4
Keeping Your Financial Records Tidy

The reliability and the usefulness of your QuickBooks data depends on the tidiness and neatness of your financial records. Here are four tips that will help you do a better job of maintaining your financial records.

> **Resolve your QuickBooks bank accounts regularly**

When you take some time for reconciling a bank account, you are not only improving the precision of your bank account, but you are also able to indirectly check a lot of transactions, such as all the transactions for the flow of revenue into a bank account and the expenses flowing out of a bank account on a regular basis.

Keep updating loan account balances

If you have borrowed any money from a bank, then it would be wise to keep regularly checking the balance of that account. If it isn't the same as the one in the lender's records by the end of the year you should update it. Loan accounts tend to go wrong over a period of time because the calculations of principal and interest can be slightly off and this error keeps snowballing over a period of time. It is really easy to fix the balances in this account; all that you will have to do is add a journal entry to fix any problem and correct the necessary debit or credit to even out the discrepancy.

Check for any orphan payments

People tend to overlook a very simple entry. After receiving payments from a customer, they forget to enter the same to the invoice. This is an error of omission and when this occurs, your revenues are understated in your Profit and Loss statement. You can detect these orphan payments by producing a cash basis balance sheet in your QuickBooks file. If this balance sheet shows a negative balance for your accounts receivable, then this would indicate you have entered some payments into the QuickBooks but haven't entered the payment on the invoice. To fix this error, you will have to go through your customer's payments or the list of transactions done by a customer to find such an omission.

Review your balance sheet regularly

A balance sheet is the one place where all the accounting errors show up. For this very reason, it would be helpful if you would make it a habit to keep producing a balance sheet on a regular basis. Look for numbers that don't seem normal; for instance, if your undeposited funds total to $40,000, this would mean you have a total of $40,000 lying around somewhere. You can double-check such odd values by going through the transaction data that adds up to a wrong value. One last point you should keep in mind is about the technique of checking errors. Often the error that produces a crazy value in your balance sheet isn't a wrongly entered transaction, but it could be a transaction that has been overlooked altogether.

Tips for dealing with deposits in QuickBooks

If you are using QuickBooks, then you will have to deal with deposits. In this chapter, let us take a look at a cash flow technique and the bookkeeping important for this particular technique. A simple way for improving your cash flow is to take upfront deposits or retainers before you start the actual work for your client or customer. This means you have to collect cash before you start the work. These customer deposits tend to create bookkeeping trouble. The question this raises is, how should you record a particular transaction for which either check or cash has been deposited, but the product or service hasn't yet been delivered? There are two options for dealing with such a situation and these are as follows:

The easy route:

You can decide to just record the sales receipt for a particular service or product. All you need to do is count the cash that is flowing into the business and then recognize the revenue. You will need to ensure that such a deposit is nonrefundable and for the purposes of cash flow, the deposit needs to be nonrefundable. You will need to count the revenue whenever you receive such a deposit if you are a cash basis taxpayer.

The Precise Way:

The second way in which you can deal with such a deposit is to treat it as a liability. When you do this, you are creating an entry in the journals that would record the cash you have received by increasing the amount of cash in the cash account, which also records the corresponding increase in the Customer Deposits current liability account. This method should be used if you are a cash basis taxpayer and the deposit is refundable or if you are an accrual basis taxpayer. Whenever the sale is completed and you have sent an invoice, then deduct the same amount from the Customer Deposit item and apply it to the invoice balance that's due.

Financial Tips for Business Owners

Business owners need to be active when it comes to the financial aspect of the business so they can foresee any efforts at embezzlement, forgery, or any other activity that would cause losses to the business. You will need to keep reviewing your QuickBooks financial statements, check the transactions to know where your money goes, and also the person who handles your finances. Here are some financial tips that might come in handy.

Nothing against bookkeepers, but in a small business, people tend to have the opportunity for easily committing frauds. When you sign all the checks on your own, you get to keep track of the cash flowing out of your business. Yes, this practice can be slightly cumbersome, but it's better to be safe than sorry. This is where QuickBooks comes in handy. Only you or an authorized person can sign the checks on your behalf. You will need to have a clear and distinctive signature and when you are scanning and uploading your signature to QuickBooks, make sure it's legible and clear. You should double check the bank reconciliation statement.

If you don't handle this on your own, make sure you review the work that has been done by the person who regularly maintains this. You don't have to hire a bookkeeper if you are making use of QuickBooks. In fact, anyone can make use of QuickBooks for maintaining your accounts even if you aren't familiar with accounting systems. Keep regularly reviewing your financial statements and take a look at the profit and loss statements prepared by QuickBooks. Make it a habit to keep checking your balance sheets as well as the other financial reports that will help you get an insight into the functioning of your business. You can ensure you have a strong grip on your business operations by looking at a few reports on a regular basis, probably once every week. This will not only help you spot any errors and misappropriations but it will also help you spot opportunities for improvement.

Here are the three financial reports QuickBooks prepares. These will help you understand the financial situation of your business. The profit and loss statement helps in comparing the numbers you have churned out in the current and the previous year so you can see how you are performing. The accounts receivable summary will help you see the list of clients who are yet to clear out their dues. The balance sheet is the third financial statement and this will help you in ensuring the financial position of your business by comparing your assets and liabilities.

When you are making use of QuickBooks, you will need to choose a system of accounting and that could be either cash or accrual basis. Cash basis is the system of accounting that can be used when the cash inflow represents sales and the cash outflow represents expenses. This might not be the situation in most of the business and it is suitable only for those businesses where there aren't any accrued transactions. Whenever you are buying and selling inventory, cash basis isn't the most helpful accounting system and accrual basis is better suited for your needs. So, depending upon your requirements, you can opt for a particular system of accounting. Depending upon the size of business you are handling, you can select one of the available QuickBooks versions. When you are managing a small business, it would be ideal if you would keep things as simple as possible. Keep them simple so you can easily tell whether or not your business is profitable.

Tips for Readying 1099 Forms with QuickBooks

Completing 1099 forms can be a difficult process even at the best of times. If you are trying to do them at the end of the year, then it will become even more problematic. However, with QuickBooks, you can greatly reduce the worries and hassles associated with completing 1099s. After all, all of your accounting data is already present in QuickBooks. The following is a short guide to help you out.

Getting Started:

One of the best things about QuickBooks is that you can stop your work anytime without losing any data. You simply need to save the work that you are doing, and you can pick it up right where you had left off. Keep this in mind while you are working on the 1099s.

Click on Vendors and choose Prepare 1099s. Choose the Let's Get Started option. If you have already been working on it, you can use the Continue with a 1099s option.

Review Company Details:

Review the details of your company. These details are important. After all, the name of your company along with its legal filing address will be used to fill up the name and address of the payer on the 1099 form. Your tax ID will also be required. Therefore, head over to the Company page and go through the details of the company. You can use the pencil icon to make changes as necessary. Any updates and changes made here will get saved to the company settings.

Assign Payments:

You will not need to assign the vendor payments to the 1099 categories. In this step, you are going to map the expense accounts in your QuickBooks to the different predefined IRS categories. The expense accounts will be those that were used for paying your vendors. Once the mapping is complete, QuickBooks will apply the payments to the appropriate boxes present on the form.

Tips:

The majority of businesses will report amounts for Box 7 only. Box 7 is Nonemployee Compensation which is about payments made for services provided by individuals who are not classified as employees. However, it is possible for you to have to report payments with a different box such as Rents or Royalties in certain cases. If you are not sure as to appropriate box, you should consult your accountant or check the IRS instructions provided for Form 1099-MISC.

Make sure that you have selected all the expense accounts that are applicable to a specific category. For example, you may have different expense accounts for the payments to various kinds of workers. For example, there might be two expense accounts named Driver Compensation and Repairman Compensation. In this case, you should select both of them when you are selecting Box 7.

Another point to remember is the reason for payment. For example, you may have paid a vendor $500 for labor and $1,000 for the equipment. In this case, you should select only the expense account that was used for paying the labor.

Confirm the 1099 Vendors:

You must now confirm the details of the vendors. This includes their names, their mailing addresses, and, finally, their tax IDs. You can click on Edit whenever you wish to update and change the details of a vendor. You may find that some vendors are eligible for 1099 but are not being displayed in the list. In this case, you can use the Select 1099 Vendors option to add them to the list. You can also use this option to remove those who are not eligible for 1099.

Tips:

When you are adding or removing vendors from the list, you will also be updating the Track payments for the 1099 setting in the corresponding vendor profile.

It is possible that you may find a vendor who is not eligible for 1099 for the current year. You should not worry about it as the list can be filtered when you are reviewing the 1099 payments and vendors.

Review the 1099 Payments and Vendors:

After making all the entries, you must always review the payments. You need to ensure that they have been assigned to the right boxes in the 1099 form.

By default, you will find that QuickBooks will be showing the 1099 vendors who have met the IRS threshold for the current tax year. You can certainly see the vendors who have been paid in an earlier tax year, have not been marked for the 1099s or whose total payments are below the IRS thresholds. In order to view them, you will have to click on the filter icon and change the settings.

You can also click on the name and make edits and updates to the vendors who are missing certain details.

Tips:

You can print a summary to keep for your own records.

If you are confused or wondering about the IRS thresholds, you can view them through QuickBooks. You simply need to move your mouse over the box number so as to view the IRS threshold for that specific category.

You can click on any amount present in the Excluded column so as to view any payments that have been made by credit cards, debit cards or even third party payment systems like PayPal. These kinds of payments will be reported the third party systems and card issuers with Form 1099-K. As such, you must prevent payments from being reported twice to the IRS. This can be done by ensuring that the 1099-MISC forms contain only direct deposits, cash, checks, ACH and EFT payments. Don't worry as QuickBooks will automatically track the right types of payments for you.

Click on any amount present in a Box column in order to open the report of 1099 Transaction Detail by Vendor. This report will show all the transactions that are a part of that amount. The additional details you can find here include the transaction type, the expense account, the date and any descriptions. You can use the back button of the browser to go back to the Review window once you have completed taking a look at the Report.

File the 1099s:

Once you have completed the preparation of the 1099s, you are ready to deliver them to the corresponding vendors while filing with the IRS at the same time. QuickBooks allows you to choose the filing method you are comfortable

Ralph McKinnon

with. Remember that each option has its own fees and charges.

Chapter 5
Basic Troubleshooting

When something goes wrong with QuickBooks, chances are it will scare you. Don't worry; most of the common problems users tend to face on QuickBooks have simple solutions. QuickBooks is a very important tool that helps you in running your business and it helps you perform all financial and accounting functions like organizing your funds, payment to your employees and vendors, receipt of deposits, and so on. QuickBooks is indeed helpful software but it can also be slightly complicated. This complexity means there are chances of it being prone to problems. In this chapter we will take a look at some of the common issues you might face when you are using QuickBooks.

Update the data file failures:

This can be a tricky problem. Whenever you are upgrading the QuickBooks from one version to another one, at times the data files stored on the earlier version cannot be read by the newer versions of QuickBooks. Because of all this, the data file will have to be updated. This usually takes place during the process of installation itself and it will require you to first create a backup. However, to avoid any issues with the data file, make sure you have run a verification of this file before you have uninstalled the previous version or have installed the latest version. There is another option you can consider; you can install the new version and let the previous version just exist on your system. This way, you will have something to fall back on.

When rebuilding of the data file fails:

Even after you have verified the data, at times the failed data file might not have been upgraded to the latest version. In such a case you should go back to the previous version and rebuild your data. For some users this might be an easy task, but it might not be so easy for others, especially when such a file contains all the company's vital financial information. If you find yourself in such a situation where you need to rebuild your data, then follow a few simple steps. You will first need to back up your data file, verify the concerned data file, and then rebuild it. If the rebuild option isn't working out for you, then you might want to take a look to make sure the data file that you are looking for is actually located on the machine in question. QuickBooks is particular that the data file needs to be located on the C: drive. This means that even if your data file is on Q: drive and it is shared, QuickBooks would assume that it is in a new drive and is not recognizing the file. This could be the reason or an issue with the rebuild. So, before you consider rebuilding your file, make sure that the copy of the data file is present on C: drive. Once the rebuild is completed you can transfer it back to whichever drive on which it was originally located.

You have lost connection to the data file:

This is perhaps the most common issue, as well as the most challenging problem to troubleshoot. QuickBooks is quite finicky about the network connection to the data file. Even if there is a slight problem with the network, your connection could be potentially lost. If you are sure your QuickBooks has been set up properly, then you can make use of the QuickBooks Connection Diagnostic Tool to help you figure out the problem. Also, ensure that you connection is able to get through both your firewall and your antivirus program.

The reinstall fails:

If you want to consider the option of reinstalling QuickBooks, then there is something you should know: the process of the clean uninstall. Before you get started with this process, you should go ahead and uninstall it by making use of the standard method of uninstallation provided by Windows. Then you will have to go back and delete the file completely from the C: drive as well as the one that exists in the documents and settings of your Windows user. You will need to back up your data before you consider a clean uninstall.

When on multiuser mode they are slow:

This is a tricky problem to troubleshoot because there could be multiple reasons causing QuickBooks to slow down. If you have managed to rule out the hardware as an issue, then the problem might actually be with your data file. The fastest way to ensure this is solved is by making use of the "Clean Up Company Data" tool present in "File

Utilities." If this doesn't help boost the speed of the program, then you can always make use of the "Audit Trail" feature.

The client machine on QuickBooks isn't able to locate a data file on the server:

The first thing you will have to do is ensure the Server Manager is installed on the system and that it is running properly. If this doesn't help, then map the drive to the server from the client and try to reconnect to it in this manner. Mostly, you will be able to see the server from the client, and then the issue would be the Server Manager isn't running.

Unable to find the licensing information:

If you have lost the documentation that came along with the software and you aren't able to find the license or product numbers, then you can find them by simply pressing [F2] or [Ctrl] + 1 when the QuickBooks is open and you have logged into your data file. If you have to reinstall, you will have to reregister.

A new printer will not print:

This is a very simple problem and it can be easily fixed but still manages to confuse many users. You will need to close QuickBooks and then search for a file named qbprint.qbp. Now, you will have to rename this file to qbprint.qbp.old. Then, restart QuickBooks. You should be able to get started with your printing work.

You've lost the admin password:

Well, this happens more frequently than you would like to think. Or perhaps you are just a new administrator who has come into a tricky situation where the old admin forgot to leave a password. Don't you worry as this is an easily fixable problem. You can retrieve the password by making use of the QuickBooks "Automated Password Reset Tool. This isn't a 100% foolproof method, but it does work most of the time.

You aren't able to copy or even move the QuickBooks data file:

For the purpose of migration or backup, have you tried to copy the QuickBooks data file from your hard drive to any other removable drive, only to discover that the file has been locked? Well, the answer to this problem is simple. QuickBooks Server Manager and Directory Monitor have the file locked away. So, close QuickBooks and click the Start menu. Select Run and enter services.msc. Look for all the QuickBooks services and then stop those two services that are running. Once you have stopped these services, then you will be able to copy and paste the files for the purpose of backing them up.

These basic troubleshooting techniques will help you conquer any minor hurdles. Just read through the troubleshooter guide to figure out what you are likely to face when you are using QuickBooks. Just remember, you don't need to panic when something isn't functioning as you will be able to troubleshoot it.

Ralph McKinnon

Chapter 6
Ten Common Mistakes To Avoid When Using QuickBooks

Getting Started:

One of the things for which QuickBooks is famous is how simple it is for everyone to use. It is an excellent choice for anyone who wants to start a business or become their own boss, and who may not have the time or capital to hire an outside bookkeeper. In the past, small businesses had to depend on an accountant or some other form of help when it came to managing the books for their business. This situation had the potential to cost a lot of money or slow the start of the business itself. With QuickBooks, just about anyone can pick up the software and get a move on setting up the books for one's company. However, this is where the problem lies. Even with access to QuickBooks, there is a learning curve, and sometimes, businesses and individuals make common mistakes before completely learning to use the program with full functionality. Although some of these errors are small and there is little to no damage done, that may not always be the case. A mistake, when serious enough, could break a small company. These cases are uncommon but they can and do happen often enough to avoid them. In the section below, you will be shown some of the potentially serious mistakes someone could make while using QuickBooks and the ways in which to avoid them.

Mistake Number #1 - Be Sure To Use Your Sales Tax Correctly

Sales taxes are placed on the sale or lease of goods and services in the United States. There is no uniform tax throughout the country. However, the federal government levies several national selective sales taxes on the sale or lease of particular goods and services. The taxes vary from state to state. A few areas of businesses are exempt from the general sales taxes, and it is in the interest of the business to find out if their business would enjoy any such exemption anywhere.

When it comes to sales tax, it can be tricky, especially when you have investments and projects in multiple areas. You are the face of your business as well as the boss, so you get to deal not only with your money but also with money coming into the business. You will need to account and follow up on taxes owed to the government. The issue is that your tax funds are a part of the resources you have brought in. If you are in the process of creating invoices and collecting your sales tax right away, it will make it much easier to keep track of the money. You also need to make sure you understand what is required by the state in which you work or currently operate, and how to make sure the correct items are being taxed when needed. When you make sure to account for sales tax from the start, you lower the risk of not having the tax money owed to the government when needed. This section will be a broad overview of common mistakes and how to fix them. So, if you are interested in getting into the gritty details, there are several places to search online to help you gain a better understanding.

The main reason the majority of people have trouble keeping track of what taxes go where is because all of their tax money is held in one spot. When you bring in money,

QuickBooks puts it all into one account. What you need to do is create a sales tax account. This way, all the sales taxes you owe are ready when you need them, be it by the end of the day, week, or even the end of the month. You could hand in your taxes yearly, but that is a massive undertaking, and you may not find everything you need at that point. So, be aware it is best to deduct sales tax right away and not risk the chance of coming up short at the end of the year. Getting into a routine is an excellent idea, and you should stick to it until you are frequently deducting your taxes. It may sound tedious, but deducting them daily, especially if you have a thriving business, is the best option. Of course, if you were only getting your income once a week, weekly would be just fine. At this point, you'll need to create an entry to move whatever amount of money you can allocate to the sales tax account in order to keep it aside.

How about an example? Say your business flourished for one day and brought in almost $20,000. You will want to check your report, commonly found in your POS system, to see how much sales tax is due. You will use that number to determine the amount of money to be placed into your sales tax account and move it there as soon as possible. Two of the biggest mistakes you can make while handling your sales tax is to include the tax as part of your sales at the end of the year or to treat them as your expenses. If you do either of these, you risk the possibility of losing a large amount of money, money that could be used for growing your business.

Some of you may be thinking, what if I were to include it in the sales and as an expense? Technically, this might work, but it is not the proper way of handling your sales tax. If you do this while operating in an area that requires sales tax, then you will end up overpaying. So, from the beginning, it is best to allocate your sales tax in the correct area, which will allow you to correctly handle your business and prevent you from paying or losing anything.

Mistake Number #2: If You Have Loans, Make Sure That You Are Properly Handling Them

If you are fortunate enough to operate your business without the help of loans, then this section may not be a big priority for you. However, most businesses, especially newer and smaller companies, tend to have loans. If this is true for you and your business, then this is a critical section to which you should pay attention. More than half of all small businesses have some loans, and it is essential you track them correctly, because in QuickBooks, most users go about this incorrectly.

These loans could entail any situation. It could be a loan for work vehicles, a loan for the building in which your business is operating, or an SBA loan used when you first buy the company you are currently running. Loans are generally repaid in parts, and these payments are not to be skipped, although sometimes people inadvertently skip them. Loans work by providing you with funds. The funds become your beginning balance. You have a principle for repayment and an interest amount you need to keep a track of in your books. Your loan should never appear entirely on the Profit and Loss Statement, unless it is an interest only loan. The most common part of the loan seen by the customer is the payment itself. This is quite obvious because it is the amount you are paying. However, there are parts you do not see unless you already have prior experience with this section. Everyone starts with an original balance. It is the amount of money you borrowed, and it is what needs to be paid back. Once the initial balance is entered, you will want to figure out how many payments you have to make and what rate of interest you are paying. If you have this information, you will be able to use a loan calculator that will be able to tell you how much each payment is going to be with interest, and how much the actual principal amount remains. Only one amount goes to the bank, despite there being two parts split in the books. The interest amount you are paying is an expense, however, the principal is not. Many people make the mistake of entering in the entire amount of the loan as an expense, and this will lead them to believe they understand their profit, and sometimes even think they will not owe as much on their taxes, but this has never been further from the truth.

Here is an example. Let's say you are paying about $500 a month on a car loan you are using strictly for business. After you do the math, you will understand how much is the principal and how much is the interest. If you enter the entire payment as an expense, it will reduce your profit, which would be incorrect on your books. On the other hand, if you just put the balance of the loan, you would miss a chance for a deduction when it comes to putting your interest in as an expense.

However, let's say you do not know the entire number of payments or the payment amount will vary over time. In that case, it is a safe thing to put the whole payment toward the loan balance on the sheet. When you get the statement from the holder of the loan that shows you the amount of interest that has been paid up until that point, you can split the total and input it as an expense on QuickBooks. You could even go as far as estimating the amount and later modify it to the appropriate amount once you figure out the exact figure reported as an expense. However, this is frowned upon, and it is always best to input the correct numbers and go about things the safe way when it comes to your money. There is never a better way to run your business than the safe way.

So, if you do happen to have a loan, make sure you know the starting balance, and see if your payments are being split between the interest and the principal. You want to ensure the principal amount is allocated to the loan account and make sure the interest amount goes to the expense account. Also, be sure to put the current loan balance on the balance sheet. Make sure anything that has been mentioned in the above section is not happening. If it is, make sure it is fixed so you can bring in the maximum amount of profit for your business.

Mistake Number #3 - You Are Not Reconciling Your Accounts

For those of you who might not understand what reconciling your accounts means, it is the process in which you match your transactions in QuickBooks with a statement usually pulled from your credit card or bank statement. This is a very straightforward yet important function you want to make sure you are doing. It allows you to make sure your balances in your bank account are the same as on the books. If these two match perfectly, then you are doing it right. If not, let's explore the modification process. It may come to a bit of a surprise, but nearly 99% of people using QuickBooks have never once reconciled their books. Reconciliation is a crucial step because if you make sure your books match and are taken care of properly, you can rest assured you are not missing anything and have no errors in your books.

The first thing to do is to see if the starting balance is correct. Then you check and double check all of your spending and deposits to make sure they are in line and are proper for that statement's period. If everything is done correctly, then your ending balance will be correct both in your books and your bank account. Many people do not follow through with this step because they believe QuickBooks is already taking care of that process through downloads. However, there are limitations to this thought process. Even if your bank accounts are being downloaded, there are times when there are errors. There are often mistakes, including improper entries, missing items, duplicates, and many other things that could be caught by reconciling your books.

If you are not downloading transactions from your banks, the chances of mistakes and major expenditures are even greater, and you may not even realize the harm you are bringing to your business. There are also a few different ways reconciling can be used incorrectly. When you go through with a transfer, you want to make sure it is only entered once. Here is an example: say you were to download your checking account, and this shows all of your transactions you have made when moving money to a savings account. Now, let's say you go ahead and download all the information from your savings account. It will bring in the transactions from that account. What you just did was duplicate all such transactions, and you now may think you have more money, which, in actuality, is not there and this thinking could lead to problems.

Many people believe reconciling is only to be used for bank accounts, but this is not true and you should not make this mistake. Reconciling can be used for your credit card accounts, PayPal accounts, lines of credit, and anything else with a beginning and ending balance. Remember, this is your business. You should spend a little extra time to make sure everything you can do has been done. Doing this will help you reduce mistakes and helps you ensure that you have all the proper information to bring in maximum profit.

You should always reconcile active accounts that deal with clients, and we encourage all of you who are participating in this activity to make sure you are doing your books. We also encourage you to make it a habit of doing this frequently. Many businesses find it best to reconcile their books at the end of the day, but this depends on the business. Smaller companies can get away with it for a few days, but it is a good habit to start reconciling every day. Once it is a habit, you'll realize it is much easier for everyone involved. If you are someone who has not reconciled your books yet, there is a good chance there are errors on these books. It would be best to look these over and to make sure everything is correct.

Now, when you do move forward and begin reconciling your books, know everything should line up and match in the end. QuickBooks is very kind and gives you an easy way to input a reconciliation discrepancy. It is the amount that should be there and what is not in there. Be sure to remember that simply locating the problem is not enough, you have to apply a solution. Be sure to fix the discrepancy or find out where it is or what is causing it. If you have come to the point where you are frequently using the discrepancy account to cover up your differences, then there is little point in reconciling in the first place.

Now, when you are reconciling, you might find there are items that have not yet cleared your bank. You should also know the average is around 30 days for credit transactions and about 60 days for checks. If this is the case, you should pull them out and clear them away because there is a good chance they will never clear. Always do some investigating as to why they may not have cleared your account. It is always best to check on this. The reason it is so important to check up on these things is that these items will lower your balance, and sometimes inflate your account in QuickBooks, even though they have not cleared at the bank. All in all, they are only messing up your end balance.

With every version of QuickBooks, this feature may change and vary. It is best to figure out exactly how your version works. Also, be sure you are reconciling each account at least once a month. It is the only way to ensure that there are no errors and that everything is correctly tallying. Make sure the ending and starting balances are correct. Reconciling is very easy and extremely fast if you do it often and make sure your books are clean. If you often find issues and are unsure of what exactly to do, there is nothing wrong with asking for help and figuring out what the problem is. Be sure to learn how to fix the issues so you can be up to date and confident at what you are doing.

Mistake Number #4 - You Are Not Using the Chart of Accounts in the Correct Manner

Chart of Accounts (COA) is a critical feature in QuickBooks, and everyone should see this feature as the foundation for their accounting. Many people miss this feature, which negatively affects them. The COA (Chart of Accounts) is a list of places where you can put your money. The primary purpose and goal for your COA is that it should be as detailed as possible to make sure you can locate information you need. However, you may want to make sure you are not putting in so much information it ends up bogging you down and does not add any significant value to your list. All information should add value to your books, not take any away. Now, it is important to remember this will not be the same for every person. Depending on who you are and what your business is, there may be things you will need to do differently than someone else.

The COA is the very first place anyone should look at when it comes to evaluating a new client, and it should tell you a lot right off the bat. You should be able to see the balance sheet. These balances should be in the positive or negative ranges. It should show the number of accounts present, how they are named, and if there are any sub-accounts. They should also appear in a very logical and organized way.

The charts should be very easy to read the first time you get them. If you do not need to change anything, and you can get a good overall view of everything there on first glance, then this would be considered an excellent chart. If you have a messy sheet, the chances for errors become greater, and there will be issues that will need to be accounted for. If your books take forever to do each month, it might be because of your COA. If this sheet is messy and unorganized, then there is a good chance your books are as well, and that can mean you'll have a greater degree of difficulty reconciling accounts and finishing off your books. The COA will be clean and well organized when you first start your business, so it is best to stick with the default, or at least start off with it, and branch off as you go, making sure you have control and fully understand what you are doing. One of the biggest mistakes anyone can make when it comes to their books is they do not know what they are doing. This could end up costing you your business. So, be sure to educate yourself on everything you do when it comes to your business. As your business continues to grow and expand, the greater the likelihood is that your COA will become much more evolved yet you should still spend time to organize it. Just because it is complex does not mean it should end up being messy.

Here are some of the common mistakes that occur in the COA. The first is an inconsistent use of the account numbers. Even though this is not a major issue for smaller companies, account numbers can slow you down a little bit, and this is a huge thing for larger companies. To avoid this mistake, be sure you are using the same account number every time. Be certain you are not inputting the wrong one or using a name. It is a good practice to use the full number every time.

The second mistake occurs due to older accounts. If you are not using an account you have had for a while, then it is best to get rid of it, make it inactive, or hide it. In some versions of QuickBooks, you will not be able to delete the account, but it is best to get rid of it if it is never used by your business. These reports can include the older history for the accounts even if their ending balance is zero. This can affect your books and it is best to throw them off to the side.

Older accounts are an issue, but an equally serious mistake is to be too precise with individual accounts. You may want to use a particular account just for paper supplies and printing supplies but never get to the point where one account is used solely for those supplies. When you are adding a sub name to the designated account, you are getting into a little too much detail, and it is best not to do so if you want a cleaner COA.

You should never have specific dates in your COA. If you start putting specific dates on your accounts, there is a good chance these accounts will never be used again because the dates would change. It's wise to drop the habit of being too specific or using dates with your accounts. Otherwise, these practices will end up cluttering your COA. Now, when people first start off, if they are creating accounts for everything that they do, there is a good chance they are too specific and they end up creating too many accounts. If you find yourself in a situation where you do not know where to put something you have, it is best to assume you have too many accounts. There is nothing wrong with deleting a few and combining a few accounts if things end up taking up a lot of space. In the end, this will help you figure out where everything is going and help you draft a more efficient COA.

There are several mistakes someone could make when they are not using QuickBooks correctly. Always be sure to do your homework and figure out ways to avoid all of these issues. In the long run, doing things right in the first place is extremely helpful and makes things much easier for you when it comes time to do your books.

Mistake Number #5 - You Are Not Going About Your Invoices in the Correct Way

Another major mistake many users make is that they are not correctly invoicing. There are two significant errors and plenty of smaller ones you should watch out for. First, let us define what exactly is an invoice. An invoice is a payment request for services or products. The thing about invoices is that as soon as you create one, it automatically counts as income, even if the client has not yet paid you.

The first major mistake people make when using invoices is that they create an invoice in QuickBooks, but they never go all the way to collect the payment. You may end up getting a check or have to run a credit card for the amount, whether it is a partial or complete payment, but you also have to input the payment correctly in QuickBooks. Most people will just deposit the check and call it a day. QuickBooks has been getting better and will sometimes catch when someone does this, but this is the exception, not the rule. It is always a good idea to follow up with this feature and make sure you are inputting all your information correctly. The reason this is such a huge issue is because when an invoice is brought into QuickBooks, it is accounted for as income. However, when a deposit is made into the bank, QuickBooks also reads this as a deposit. What ends up happening is the deposit is twice read as income, and even though this might look nice on the bottom line, when it comes time to pay taxes, it will look like you owe more than you actually do. The solution to this problem is a very simple one. When you get your payment, make sure you take care of the invoice and mark it as paid rather than entering it in as a deposit. That way, your accounts receivable for the customer who just paid will be zero. If it is anywhere in the positive, the payment was not received correctly, and you will need to go in and readjust what you did to make sure you are not putting in your numbers incorrectly.

The next largest mistake people make is creating unnecessary invoices. If you currently run a business where customers are paying you at the same time of their service or when they get their product, there is no need to make an invoice. You can use a sales receipt or record it as a deposit. If you have been making or currently do make this mistake, know this is not a huge problem. All that you have been doing is extra work for yourself. As long as you are inputting everything correctly and making sure you are not making your books seem like you are receiving more than you are, then you are on the right track. The only thing you truly risk by inputting an invoice when you don't need one is increasing the chances of a mistake. This duplication of efforts may end up being an inconvenient and unnecessary mess.

The biggest take away from this section is that you shouldn't bother with unnecessary invoices. There is no sense in creating more work for yourself than necessary and risking the chance of mistakes. While these are the two primary issues when it comes to misusing invoices, a few others include not correctly setting up and collecting sales tax, using items in the wrong place, and incorrectly writing off debt. Some of these issues do depend on the situation that you are currently in, so it is best to be vigilant when you are doing things to make sure you know what you are doing when it comes to inputting your numbers.

The way you will find out if you are making mistakes in this area is when you look at the total in your accounts receivable and balance sheet; if those numbers do not make any sense to you, then there is a good chance you are making mistakes somewhere in your invoicing. You will want to make sure you fix any and all mistakes before tax time.

So, make sure you are correctly inputting your invoices. There is no reason to create invoices if you are receiving payment at the time of purchase. If you do need to create an invoice, be sure that when you deposit the money you do not forget to go all the way with the bill. It will lead to the chance of you saying you made more money than you did and could lead to you paying more taxes than what you should have to pay.

Mistake Number #6 - You Are Not Including Your Credit Card Expenses

Now that we are in the great digital age, we can access our funds instantly, with ease, and in many ways. Credits cards allow all business owners immediate access to money. As a business owner, technology gives you the ability to immediately pay off your balances or earn reward points on your existing credit cards. Technology truly gives you the ability to take control of your money and improve profits if used in a smart way. However, like anything else, problems can arise with credit cards if you do input the charges as expenses. In fact, this is a significant opportunity you should definitely take into consideration and implement into your business strategy. More often than not, people are making payments and these reports go into the bank, but then there are no corresponding expenses. When you are not entering your credit card payments and are not giving them corresponding expenses, you are shortchanging yourself on your deductions. You are entitled to these deductions from your income and it is an excellent idea to start doing this if you want to bring in more money.

The first thing you want to make sure is that your accounts are not Amex because these are not recognized for the most part. In fact, all of your credit cards should be set up through credit card accounts. You want to make sure these are not expense reports. Of course, there are always exceptions to these rules, but remember to make sure you know your situation and go about this process in the way you should. One of the reasons is that someone is using a card directly for advertising and nothing else. As long as this card is solely for publicity, there is no interest and no annual fee. This will allow you to input this number safely.

This is a very special exception because only a few people use credit cards in this manner. Almost all businesses use their cards to buy lunch, tickets, gas, and many other small things for their business. There is nothing wrong with using their cards for these kinds of expenditures, but it is always best to allocate them to their various accounts. The biggest thing to remember when using your card for these sorts of expenses is to make sure you are breaking down where the card was used, that way you can track of all of your money.

After all of that, here is the easiest solution when it comes to quickly setting up your account in QuickBooks. It is to use the download function and directly pull and label your transactions. This way, all of your expenses are correctly tracked and the month in which they were made is on record. You won't have unaccounted for payments. Another reason this becomes such an important part of everything you are doing is to know the differences in the payment because you will be accounting it differently. When you are going to pay, say six thousand dollars in payments, but in reality, you have almost fifteen thousand to be paid, you should know what the extra expenses are and get all those expenses as a credit. If these are missing from your book, then you risk not collecting some of your benefits.

While some of the information in this section may be confusing, here is basically what you need to know when it comes to including your credit card expenses. If you have a credit card you are currently using for your business, make sure that you enter any and all expenditures to the credit card account. Then be sure those payments that are on that card are going directly to the primary credit card account from the bank account you are using to make payments. For each of your expenses, you need to make sure that it is charged on the card and that you input the correct amount of the cost each time. If you do this, you will add a charge, and then the balance in the account linked to the credit card should go up with that amount. Then, when the time comes for you to look at the report assessment, the current balance on the statement for the credit card should be the same as what it is in the statement for the credit card for the same date. Be sure to add or subtract any pending transactions. If your numbers are not remotely near the same or if you see you are deeply in the negative, then you will want to make sure you have inputted all of your data correctly, because somewhere there are major problems you need to fix in order for your books to accurately reflect your business.

How often should you be doing this? You should be doing this for every credit card you are using for your business. When the statement is generated online or it arrives in the mail, you should be busy filing and keeping records. The next thing you do is to make sure you reconcile the accounts with the credit cards. It is the safest and the only way to make sure all of your entries are entirely correct.

Mistake Number #7 - You Are Not Tracking Your 1099s Correctly

When you are a small enough business, or you are self-employed, there is little need for individual forms. However, when you grow into bigger companies that need to keep track of all of their employees and outside contractors, you will need to understand this: it is imperative you monitor all of your 1099 forms. These forms are issued to certain companies or individuals that provide services that add up to six hundred dollars or more in total payments for that accounting year. Corporations and employees are not involved in these forms for product purchases. Very few LLCs are exempt. There are rules to follow when it comes to helping you figure out what forms you need to fill. Just know it changes a little bit every year and depends on who qualifies. The thing is, you can do yourself a huge favor if you get ahead of the game and start tracking from the very beginning. If you make this conscious effort, you should be tracking who you are involved with, business-wise, if they require a 1099 and if they do, request they provide you with a completed W-9 form. This process is extremely crucial. The safest way for you to obtain it is to hold onto their payment until the vendors or individuals have provided you with this information. These forms are very simple and do not take long to fill out, so there should be no reason for them not to promptly comply with your request. They will gladly fill it out if they know their check is on the line.

Now, there are cases where certain people do not allow you to give them a 1099 form. If this is the case, you are left with a decision. If you do not give a 1099 to someone who is eligible for the form, you still have to clear the expense and then you put yourself at risk for potentially not being able to use it as an expense if you are caught and audited.

By issuing this form to the party who provided you the required services, you are providing proof you paid them for their service, and this tells the government they should look for income taxes from that person and not you. If you do not issue the 1099 form, the government can step in and claim the payment, which may not have been paid. If this were the case, you, therefore, would end up owing income tax on the payment because it will look like you used it to lower your net profit. This is an enormous issue because every year these forms are to be sent out by the last day of January. Sometimes this does not line up with the payments that will be received over that period. So, by the time all the payments are made, you may only have a short amount of time to get all of the 1099 info filed and put together. If you do not go ahead and fill out your books or if you don't identify your vendors early on, there is a very high chance none of it will get done at all. That is why it is paramount to do this early on because if you decide to leave it for later, there is a good chance it will be tough to get all this done in time. This seems to be a colossal problem when it comes to those who use QuickBooks.

So, be sure to study well when it comes to working with 1099 forms. Be sure that if you have someone else taking care of this process for you that you proofread his or her work completely. There is always a chance an outside agency or accountant can make mistakes. The best way to go about this issue is to make a list of all of your vendors who are currently active and identify which ones are eligible for a 1099 form. If you do not have a W-9 form for this vendor, you need to make sure you get one from them immediately, especially if you have already compensated them for several payments. Hold off on any future payments until a W-9 form is handed back to you, so you do not have to pay for income tax yourself. With their account, be sure to mark it as 1099 eligible. Some of your vendors might take longer to get to than others, and some vendors do not even meet the $600 requirement. However, for those who do meet this requirement, it is much easier for you to keep track of this stuff early on and it will keep you on the right side when it comes time to fill out your taxes. By following this process, you can get ahead of the January deadline and make sure you do not fall behind.

Mistake Number #8 - You Are Not Using Your Assets Correctly

Most assets tend to remain on your books for a long time. When it comes to controlling and managing your assets, there are very precise definitions applied to them in accounting. The issue is that most people do not understand or realize this, and this is one of the most common areas where mistakes tend to happen when it comes to handling your assets. There is the common misconception that assets are simply things you possess, but when it comes to the accounting world, as it does when you are working in QuickBooks, this is not accurate enough.

The first types of assets are fixed assets. Commonly speaking, these are the things that hold material value, such as a physical presence and something that has an expected life of one or more years at your business. An excellent example of this is the building from which you are currently operating. This is a fixed asset and it is usually taken into consideration if it is worth more than five hundred dollars and has a lifespan of over a year, at the least.

A worst possible example of something that has been recorded as a fixed asset would be a box of paper clips. Yes, this is a physical material in your business, but it does not meet the other requirements of a fixed asset. There is a good chance those paper clips will not make it through the year. In addition to paper clips, other examples of things not commonly considered fixed assets are small tools, office supplies, small parts, and everything else that does not meet the standard requirements for fixed assets. Something else that may need clarification as not a fixed asset is a patent within a company. It may gladly reach the dollar limit and be around for at least a year, but it is currently not a physical element that exists in the company. Many things commonly found as fixed assets are buildings, equipment, and even furniture. Another thing many companies can claim as fixed assets are vehicles. However, be aware you can only claim vehicles that were purchased outright. Leased vehicles do not count as fixed assets. When you go out and buy a vehicle, you get to put your total expenditure in your books as a fixed asset. If there is a loan, however, the loan is entered separately in QuickBooks as a liability. If you find yourself in the situation where you have to lease space and invest money in repairs for something or even the rearranging of your business, those totals and costs for that kind of work can be tracked as a separate tenant-improvement asset.

There are different types of assets. If an asset is not a fixed asset, it can fall into different kinds of categories. There are categories for patents, trademarks, licenses, non-tangible items, and franchise fees. Most of what is not a fixed asset will fall into one of these areas. Most small businesses have next to none or maybe just a few different kinds of assets. So, if you look around and do not see anything, then you are most likely fine. However, if you find yourself with many different kinds of assets, you probably have a very different and unusual business, or you are looking at things in the wrong way. The best way to decide whether an individual item is a certain kind of asset is to do some research and get a list of what qualifies and what does not.

Now, when it comes to the inventory within your business, this does count as a different type of asset. It is a specialized category and consists of all the things you have bought for the firm and intend to sell or resell. This includes products you purchased completely to sell as is, or a product that must be assembled. When it comes to your inventory, there is no bottom line when it comes to a dollar amount. If you have something that is only worth half a penny, it can still count toward your inventory. However, when it comes to stocking the material, there are time constraints you must follow. Of course, it all depends on what you are selling, but there is a chance that everything or a particular item in your inventory is completely gone, or if there is a chance you will not be able to sell or resell it, then you need to adjust the value of your inventory status.

So, when the time comes for you to take control and manage all of your assets, you want to be sure that you know what belongs where. When it comes to fixed assets, remember there is a dollar limit, a time limit, and it has to be something that is a physical part of your business, for example, the building, vehicles, and so on. Be sure that you know the difference so you can help yourself avoid any problems later on. When it comes to particular types of assets, almost everything else falls into the "other" asset category unless you are running a specialized business. Then there are inventory assets. If something is about to go out of style or there is the chance a product has spoiled, is not fit for sale, or anything of that nature, be sure to take it off your inventory sheet. It will help in the long run. Remember, there is no bottom dollar amount when it comes to recording your inventory assets. Although, be sure to keep in mind there is a slim constraint. These are items bought with the intention of being sold or resold and parts that are to be assembled into a different product that will once again be sold.

Go through all of your fixed asset accounts. Be sure to add in anything you might have missed or remove anything you did not realize was not worth enough or around long enough to be considered a fixed asset. Also, be sure anything that is on that account is still around. If you are keeping track of items that are no longer around, you might be in trouble when it comes to doing your taxes. Make sure everything on your books is entirely accurate. If you find out there are inconsistencies with what you own and what your books say, you might land into problems later on.

Mistake Number #9 - You Are Not Handling Your Payroll in the Correct Manner

One of the essential functions of QuickBooks is also one of the easiest to master. The program to manage payrolls is probably one of the most used functions of the program, simply because most business owners will have employees whom they need to pay. However, the number of people who do not use or understand this concept is pretty high. It is essential you, as a small business owner, understand how to use this function in QuickBooks.

One of the first and most common errors people will make is they put items into payroll that do not belong there, as they do not meet the classification for payroll entries. How do you know which items to put into payroll? Think of it this way, if you have to take taxes or individual withholdings out of an employee's check and that employee has filed a W-4 form, then this meets the requirements for a payroll entry. Payments issued to employees will not always be called paychecks, though that is a common misconception for many business owners.

Here is why this is such a severe issue. If you find yourself in a situation where you issue a check to someone, and you are not withholding taxes on that payment, or if you are filing them as payroll payments and not paying payroll taxes, you are going to be the one that will end up on the wrong side of the IRS as well as with the state department. There is an exception, however, if you live in one of the states that does not require payroll taxes.

If you are paying someone to perform an individual service and you are not creating the correct paycheck for him or her, then that payment, along with the person who is acquiring that paycheck, will more than likely qualify for Form 1099. One way to figure out how all of this works is to make sure you are treating this person the way you should—as an employee or as an independent contractor. If they are meant to be an employee, then you are the one who needs to make sure he or she is receiving appropriate payments while you are taking out the taxes. However, if this person is not familiar enough to be an employee, you should be giving him or her a 1099 form along with their payment, because this is not payroll and you are not taking money out for taxes. They will need to be the ones to take the taxes out. Basically, if you are telling someone when and how to work, and where they need to be working, along with providing them the tools and resources that they need, such as work clothes, desks, computers, among other things, then you should consider this person as an employee and you, by law, are required to give them a paycheck in which taxes are withheld and taken out by you.

On the other hand, if the person you are receiving services from does not work at your location and they are in control of when they work and are required to provide their own resources such as equipment and tools, then they would be considered a 1099 contractor. If this is the case, you are to give them a payment that is not a payroll check and the taxes are not withheld. If these people have their business license, work for many other employees besides you and can provide their own insurance, then you are not their employer.

Now, after you have figured out which people are employees and which are not, the next step is to be able to create real paychecks. You can do all of this through QuickBooks if you have the payroll subscription, or you can use a different payment service of your choosing.

Some banks can offer payment services, but they are not knowledgeable about or required to provide you with the filings you need. They are just required to generate paychecks for you. On the other hand, there are many companies who provide full-service payrolls services, such as Paychex and ADP. They can provide you with a full suite of services but they tend to be very expensive and they don't offer much flexibility. If you are a smaller business, it is almost better to learn how to go about all of these processes yourself. If you are a small business, the expense is not worth it, unless you are in a very particular scenario. CapForge, though, does offer a full payroll service and is integrated into QuickBooks. It costs much less than some of those other companies and can be much more comprehensible than other banks, services, and even yourself.

However and whatever way you decide to go about this process, make sure you study and understand all the rules. If you fail to be honest and are unable to pay the correct payroll taxes when they are due, there are penalties. Furthermore, not paying your employees can lead to very hefty fines that can cripple your business. There are stiff penalties that will also come from state labor boards, so keep in mind this is not something that should be taken lightly. It is, in fact, a very serious matter that needs your full attention.

When it comes down to it, the first thing you should understand is the definition of a paycheck and how that figures into QuickBooks. If you are taking taxes out, then it is a paycheck. If you are only handing out a check and not taking taxes out, then you need to be sure that if it is over $600, you give that person or business a 1099 form to make sure you do not end up paying the taxes at the end of the year. Next, once you understand the differences between a paycheck and a payment for services, you need to know who are actual employees in your business. The ones who are not will need to be listed as contractors. Contractors need to be inputted in QuickBooks as vendors and you need to keep them separate from those of your employees. Make sure you are issuing your workers actual checks, not 1099 forms, and that these checks contain a gross pay amount, the amount of the check, the net pay amount, and any deductions. Any and all payroll taxes should be posted to your liability account. When it comes time to pay the IRS and all your state taxes, the payment should reduce the amount on your liability account, and then it will show up as an expense on your loss and profit statement.

If at any time you do not know how to properly handle your payroll, whether it is on time, each month, or as you do your quarter taxes, the penalties you have to pay are usually minuscule. If you compare these to the fines you would have to pay if you were to get in trouble, you may not have a business afterward.

Mistake Number #10 - Making Sure That You Are Using Your Equity Right

This may be a confusing section, but be sure to stick with me. It is very crucial that you understand what equity is and how to go about reporting it the correct way. Now, what is equity? Equity represents your ownership in your business. It just happens to be the section that comes right after liabilities on QuickBooks and right before the COA. Depending on the type of business you are running and taking care of your equity may vary. You may have several different equity accounts and you may even have more accounts if your company also contains investors or other business owners are involved, even if they are not taking an active role in the business.

There are several different kinds of mistakes to which you need to pay attention. The first and most major mistake people make when it comes to equity is they are not using the correct name for accounts. For every owner, in most cases, there are at least two accounts; one for putting money in and another for taking money out. The equity belonging to sole proprietors is usually called "owner equity" and "owner draw." If you are working with partnerships, it is "partner equity" and "partner draw." And for others, they have their names.

The next biggest mistake is people leave a balance in opening equity. On QuickBooks, if you are opening up the equity, a defaulted account is created to give you a place to put in a beginning balance. However, this is not a real account. So, you should not use it at all. If you do use it, you need to make a journal entry and you need to move the amount to where it all belongs. The money tends to belong to an equity account, and it typically means money invested in the business is by the owner or many owners.

Another major mistake is making a specialized account for every year for special withdrawals. There should only be two accounts for every owner. You do not want to make things more confusing by throwing in another account. This can cause serious issues and will make your records and sheets a mess. Be sure not to create sub-accounts either. If you are using equity accounts for your loans, this is a big no-no. If you put around a thousand dollars in your business, and you plan to pay yourself back later on, then it does not belong in the equity account. You should set this up as a loan from yourself to the business. Then when the business pays you back, whether it is wholly or partially, you can then record the payments in the same account. This will show the new balance if any amount is owed. If you were to do this as an equity investment and move it to distribution, you would run the risk of it looking like income, and if you do this, you are more likely to be subject to income taxes instead of a repayment for your loan. This is not a payment.

While some of that may have been confusing, you are always more than welcome to continue some further research. If you are ever concerned or confused about certain aspects of what you are doing, be sure to educate yourself. A few hours of research will always save you more money in the long run if you are doing things correctly. So, what you want to do is make sure you go through your equity accounts. Be sure you are using them the correct way. If you have not touched some of the accounts you currently have, then you need to go in and figure out how to go about it and move the money to where it belongs. If there were still money in your opening equity account, this would be the perfect time to move it to its appropriate place and to record a journal entry. Lastly, if you have multiple accounts all belonging to the same person, then you need to combine some of them so you can clear up a mess that does not need to be there.

Summary: QuickBooks is a very powerful tool and when it is used in the correct manner, it can be a great way to keep your business running smoothly. When you use QuickBooks accurately, you're giving yourself the opportunity to build and manage your business in the most efficient and reliable way possible. You're empowering yourself and your business. While we all will make mistakes due to our human nature, never get discouraged. There are many mistakes someone can make when it comes to working with QuickBooks. Hopefully from this section, you will be able to avoid some of the major ones and know how to go about fixing any that do occur to prevent your books from becoming a huge mess. If you do make a few mistakes, there are solutions in this chapter and plenty available through online resources that will help bring you to the place you need to be.

Just remember to go over this section briefly again from time to time to make sure you are correctly handling your business.

Now, the main thing to remember when it comes to all these potential pitfalls is just keeping on top of your bookkeeping can prevent them. Falling behind on their accounting is one thing many people do and it costs them in the long run. If you fall behind, many times it will be a struggle trying to rebuild the data and information about your business. When you're disorganized, you may miss deadlines or filing dates, and this could result in stiff penalties. While some major businesses can get away with this, there are many small businesses that risk falling apart and crashing completely if they have big errors in their bookkeeping.

Mistakes would and could be made using QuickBooks, but that is not the point of contention. One needs to address those mistakes and troubleshoot. You need to find that drive to get into your books and keep records of everything related to your business. Bookkeeping can be very stressful, and it is one of the least favorite things to spend time on, especially when you could be working the floor and making your business thrive. However, your company will not make it if it fails to sustain, especially because of something preventable. Another reason you need to keep up with your bookkeeping is if you stall, and eventually come around to it, you will find it can be quite challenging when everything needs to be redone at once. If you keep up to date with everything you are doing and keep track of every aspect of your business, you will be able to stay at the forefront of your business. This habit will only lead to success in being more organized, and you will be able to bring in maximum profit when it comes to the IRS and deductions. You will also be able to summon reports in your business at any time and make sure there is nothing that needs immediate and serious attention.

So be sure to keep these common mistakes in mind and also educate yourself on others. The more you know about mistakes others have made, the more cautious and informed you will be about running your business. This vigilance will also allow you to avoid mistakes altogether, or before they get too far out of hand. It will help you to reduce them in the future as well. If you made it this far, you've done a great job, and will now hopefully avoid the top ten mistakes made within QuickBooks.

Ralph McKinnon

Chapter 7
Recording Transactions In QuickBooks

How to Record Transactions in QuickBooks?

You will be able to record your deposits, checks and account transfers with the help of QuickBooks. Its register window is quite similar to a paper record which you use for keeping track on your bank account and the transactions you make. With QuickBooks, you will be able to enter your transactions into the account register directly.

To get a bank account transaction into your account register directly, you need to follow these steps.

Use the Register Command

When you choose "Banking," make sure you use the register command; QuickBooks shows the "Use Dialog" box. This "Use Register" box then asks you choose the bank account that you want to be displayed on the register.

Select the Account

After QuickBooks shows the register window, if it indicates the record of an account apart from the one that you want to see, you will have to select Banking option and then "Use Register" once again. This 'Use Register' box enables you to choose any account that you opt for. As a matter of fact, you can also select a non-bank account.

Recording the Dates

There is an MM/DD/YY format for date entry. You can enter the date of your deposit, transaction and transfer. You can also click on the small calendar button that is on the right side of the date field. This displays the month which shows the date. You then click the day button which corresponds to the date that you would like to enter.

Allocate a Transaction Number

Make use of the number column for identifying the transaction, uniquely. For example, in the case of check transactions, you have to use the "Number Field" for the check numbers. In the case of deposits and transfers, you do not have to record a number.

Recording Information in Payee Field

You can use "Payee Field" for recording the payee for a check or the customer making the payment for a deposit. In fact, it can also be used for recording other information related to transfer transaction. You should know that you can choose an existing customer, vendor or a name from one of the QuickBooks lists, just by clicking on the down-arrow button on the right end of the Payee Field. After you do this, QuickBooks will display a complete list of names. You have to click on the option that you want to select.

Provide the Transaction Amount

In case you are describing a check transaction for any transfer that moves money from your account, you will have to use the Payment column. While, on the other hand, you have to use the deposit column for describing a deposit into your account or transfer into the account. Make sure that you enter the amount in the appropriate column, payment or deposit, by using dollars and cents.

Identify Your Account

In the case of check transactions, you have to use the Account Field for the identification of an asset that a check purchases and the expense which a check pays. You have to use the "Account Field," for identifying sales revenue that the deposit represents, in the case of deposit transactions. On the other hand, for transfer operation, you have to use the Account field for identifying the other account that is involved in the transaction.

In the Account box, you will be able to enter the Account name. You can also open the Account drop-down list and then choose the account that you want.

Provide a Memo Description

If you want, you can use the Memo field for providing a brief description of the payment, transfer transaction, and the deposit.

Split Transaction

If your transaction has to be assigned to more than a single account, you have to click on the Split button. Then the QuickBooks shows the Splits area in the register window. You will be able to split your account into several accounts through the Splits area. Like a check that pays for computer repair expenses and office supplies, it can be divided in between these two accounts.

Furthermore, a deposit transaction that represents both the service revenue as well as the product revenue can be split in between these two accounts. After you are done with the Splits area, you just have to click on the close button.

You will be able to delete all the Splits details simply by clicking on the Clear button. You can use QuickBooks for recalculating the payment or the deposit amount through the split transaction data. All you have to do is to click on the Recalc button.

The Split area will also allow something that isn't possible in the regular register. You can make use of the Splits area for recording the customer's job description, billing information, and class of information. For doing this, you will have to use the Job column, the Class column, and the Billable column.

Recording the Transaction in the Register

To register an operation in the log, you will have to click on the record button. QuickBooks recalculates the balance of your account and then adjusts the ending balance for a whole new transaction.

Finding the Solution that Suits Your Business

Being a QuickBooks user, you might already be aware of the fact that it is a flexible application. However, flexibility can turn into confusion quite rapidly. Your business might have some particular needs and QuickBooks many different ways for recording the transaction. It is ready to go through the data periodically and here are some important aspects that you need to concentrate on.

Setting up a Closing Date

If you do not set a deadline, you might run the risk of recording the transactions of the previous year, unintentionally. This might lead to many problems, particularly at the year's end when you are comparing the existing balance with the issued financial statement and also the tax returns. You will get a closing date in the "accounting preferences," very conveniently. It will enable you to record the previous transaction if required. However, you will have to enter a password for doing that. It is recommended that you close it every month when the issued or internal financial statement is complete. Nonetheless, the closing date should at least be set at the end of the fiscal year.

Create Date Warning

This follows the same procedure as the setting of the end date, but it can also help in preventing the mistake of entering the transaction with a future date. This can also be found in the "accounting preferences" and through this, you will be able to set the number of days for a warning, both for the past and future dates of a transaction.

Reviewing the Internal Financial Statement and General Account Balances for Accuracy

While preparing the year-end tax returns or financial statements, there is one thing that is apparent; several account balances are not accurate. Here are some examples,

• The Accounts Receivable and the Accounts Payable aging reports fail to match the general ledger detail for a particular date.

- Record of an equipment purchase in the expense account instead of the fixed asset account.

- Record of loan payment in the wrong account.

- Payroll tax being registered in the expense account rather than the liability account.

It is extremely convenient to record a payment or a bill to a default general ledger account. With QuickBooks, things get done very quickly. Make a detailed study of the account general ledger to take a closer look at the transaction that has already been recorded. Compare the Accounts Payable as well as the Accounts Receivable aging detail with the general ledger report and then correct all the inaccuracies.

Review the Chart of Accounts

You always have to USE and REQUIRE the account numbers which can also be found in the "accounting preferences." You need to deactivate the old and unused accounts. You also need to look for all the duplicate accounts and then make one of them inactive. In case you have a slight variation in the account description, such as "office supplies expense" and "office supplies", you can clean the financial statement using just one account.

Review the Item List

You need to go through the items to see to which account the item is being recorded to as a default. This is a quite prevalent reason for an inaccurate report, but it can be easily corrected. Further, you shouldn't use the same item for bills, as well as invoices. This is because sales, as well as the cost of sales, will be recorded to the same account. Albeit, the bottom line, and net income will be the same, the sales and the costs of sales will be understated. This will lead to a discrepancy with the sales report that has been recorded on your sales tax returns when compared to your financial statements. This will also cause a problem with the tax returns and financial statement, in the case that it isn't adjusted.

Method for Entering Loan in QuickBooks

Some business might have to borrow money for funding capital investments like new premises, products and equipment research and development. When the money has been borrowed, it has to be recorded as a loan liability on the account and then tracks every loan payment that you are making for reducing the debt. With the help of QuickBooks, you will be able to set a liability account for long, as well as short-term loans, for recording and tracking the loan repayments and the loan deposit amount.

Given below are the steps that you need to follow for creating a loan liability account.

• Step One: After you have opened QuickBooks, you have to click on the tab that says "List" in the top menu and then you have to click on the option that says, "Chart of Accounts," present in the context menu.

• Step Two: Click on the button that shows "Account." It will showcase a list of accounts. Choose new from the drop down menu.

• Step Three: After this, you will have to select the company list and the "Chart of Accounts."

• Step Four: After opening the "Chart of Accounts," you have to click on any location on the list and then choose "New" from the menu. After this, select the option other from the accounts list and then you have to click on the down arrow button for expanding the list of account types that are available.

• Step Five: Click on the option that says "Other Current Liability" for loan repayment of one year or less. On the other hand, you have to click on "long-term liability" for loan repayments of long term. After you are done, click on the continue button.

• Step Six: Following this, you need to enter the name and the reference number for the accounts in the appropriate field. Keep the balance zero.

• Step Seven: Completing this you have to close it by clicking on the "Save and Close" option.

Next are the steps for creating a deposit loan account.

• Step One: For this, you need to click on the option that says "Banking," to be found in the main menu. Under this, you will find "Make Deposits." In case the Payments to the Deposit window opens up, you will have to click on the cancel button for closing it.

• Step Two: After this, you will have to select the deposit account for the loan in the window on Make Deposit.

• Step Three: Put in the name of the respective liability account which you have created for tracking the credit in the column of "From Account."

- Step Four: Next thing you need to do is to type the amount of the loan in the column that says "Amount."

- Step Five: When you are done with the entire process, you will have to save it by clicking on the save button.

After the creation of the accounts comes the primary task, recording the loan payments,

Step One: Click on the option "Banking," which you will find in the main menu and then choose the option Write Checks.

Step Two: You have to enter the name of the payee and the amount of repayment in the related field in the window of Write Checks.

Step Three: You have to assign the interest element of the loan repayment to the preferable expense account in the detail section of the window of Write Checks. You have to assign the principal which is referred to the rest of the payment to the liability account that you have made for tracking the loan.

Step Four: If you want QuickBooks to enter the payment automatically and intermittently and also issue a payment reminder then you have to click on "Edit" and then choose "Memorize Check."

Step Five: For saving the transaction, you have to select the option "Save and Close."

Ralph McKinnon

Chapter 8

Setting Up Bank Accounts And Credit Cards Through QuickBooks

How to Add Bank Accounts to QuickBooks.

Connecting your bank account to QuickBooks means it will be able to download your transactions. You have to categorize the transaction and then add it to QuickBooks. This will enable QuickBooks to start doing the work. For setting up a bank account, you will have to follow guidelines that have been given below.

Connect It to the Bank Account

On the Homepage, there is an option called Bank Accounts, under that you will find Connect an Account, click on that. Select your bank and then add the username and password that you use for accessing the account. When you are done with it, you will have to click on the "Log In" option.

Choose the Account

Once you are connected, you will be able to see all of the accounts that you have in the bank. Select the account that you use for business and then describe the type of account that it is. QuickBooks will download every transaction from the last 90 days. However, keep in mind that they aren't in QuickBooks yet.

Enter the Transaction

On the Bank and Credit Card window, you will find the option that says Category or Match column for sorting the transactions; you need to click on that. You will notice the areas in which QuickBooks tried looking for some transactions. Click on the first purchase list for opening it.

Change the Transaction Category

To put the transaction in a different category, you have to open the transaction menu and then select the right option. In case this is a new transaction, click on Add that you will find on the right side of the column.

Choose a Payee

You need to select a Payee. If it is a new payee, then you have to click on Add and then enter the name that you need to include. After this, you have to click on the Save option for saving it. You can join the rest of the details later on.

Transfer

If you made a loan payment or business credit card payment by a transaction, then open the transaction and select Transfer.

Split

In the case you have bought items from various categories through a single transaction then you have to choose Split. This will then open up the window of Split Transaction. This is where you select the appropriate categories and the amount that you are spending on each.

Batch Action

If QuickBooks categorizes a bunch of transactions correctly, then you will be able to accept them with just one click on one of the checkboxes, holding down the Shift key and then opting for the final one in the list. Open the Batch

Action window and then select Accept for accepting all of them.

Correcting a Mistake

If you include a transaction accidentally that does not belong to this batch, click on the QuickBooks tab. After this, choose the transaction and then "Undo" it. You will be able to place it in the "New Transaction" so that you can place it to where it belongs.

How to Add Credit Card Accounts to QuickBooks.

In case you want to keep track of your credit card spending and balance through QuickBooks, you will have to set up a credit card account if you haven't already done this in the QuickBooks setup. You can also use bank accounts for tracking things like money which flow in and out of savings, checking and petty cash accounts. To set up a credit card account, you will have to follow the same steps which you use for setting up a bank account.

Chart of Accounts

You can either click on "Choose List" and then on "Chart of Accounts" or you can click on the "Chart of Accounts" icon that is on the Home Screen. This then displays the window of "Chart of Accounts."

Add New Window

You have to click on the Add New Account Window on the left-hand side of the Chart of Accounts window and then select new. This will display the options buttons which correspond to the different kinds of accounts which QuickBooks allows.

Select the Option for Credit Card

You have to choose the option of QuickBooks; this will tell QuickBooks that you want to create a credit card account. After this, click on the option that says continue. QuickBooks then displays the second window for Add New Account.

Naming the Account

To provide a name in the Account Name text box, you have to move the cursor towards that box, and then you have to enter the name that is there on your credit card.

Provide the Card Number

You have to use the text box of Credit Card Acct. No. In case you are making a general Credit Card account for more than a single card; you have to leave the Credit Card Acct. No. text box unfilled. When you are doing this, you can also describe the card. You can type Usury in the text box of Description, relying upon the interest rate of the card.

Save the Details

Click on the save and close button for saving the details. After this, the QuickBooks redisplays the window of Chart of Accounts. The window now shows an additional account which is the credit card account that you have just created.

Using the Credit Card Account

After the window is being displayed, double-click on the credit card accounts that you want to use. QuickBooks then shows the Credit Card Register where you can start recording the transactions.

You can also click on the "Enter Credit Card Charges" icon in the Banking section of the Home screen, instead of the "Chart of Accounts" window. As a matter of fact, you can also click on "Banking" and then "Enter Credit Charges."

Reasons for Connecting Accounts to QuickBooks

Connecting the bank accounts as well as the credit card accounts to QuickBooks will help you to do much less manual data entry, agile account balancing and also helps you to be ready during tax time.

Connecting Bank Accounts

When you connect the bank accounts, QuickBooks helps you to keep a track of all the ATM withdrawals and purchases. Furthermore, it also keeps a note of all online money transfers. Rather than entering every single transaction methodically, you can download them directly from the bank; this helps you to save time.

Connecting Credit Card

If you are sharing your business credit card with your colleagues, then organizing the receipts of everyone can be a difficult task. When you are connecting your credit card with the accounts of QuickBooks, you will be able to download all the purchases without bothering who has purchased what.

Reconciling Made Convenient

Reconciling accounts is a laborious task that small scale business owners have to deal with. Once you are connecting your accounts to QuickBooks, each time you are working with the download transactions, you are teaching QuickBooks about the business. QuickBooks will now be able to recognize the transactions on your behalf. This will help you to save time. When you have to file for your business, the transaction will already be categorized, and this makes reconciling quite convenient.

Chapter 9
Guide To The Interface Of QuickBooks

Bank Feeds: The Online Banking Center

To get the Bank Feed menu, you have to go to the Banking menu. This will then lead you to Bank Feeds under which you will find Bank Feeds Center. This is used for keeping your account up-to-date. For synchronizing the transaction with the financial institution, you will have to click on the Refresh Account.

The window of the transaction list will allow you to match the downloaded transaction with the existing ones in the account register and then add up your new transactions.

Display Modes

Express Mode is QuickBooks default Online Banking interface. It has changed a great deal when compared to the side-to-side mode online banking interface. This is a brand new interface, and this offers better workflow and provides better visuals for showcasing the customer data. The first time that you set up an account for online banking, you will be asked to set the display mode. This is either Register Mode or the Express Mode. Express Mode is the new mode with some advanced features.

You will have to select the Help menu and then click on QuickBooks Help. After this, you will have to search for Online Banking Modes and then choose the Online Banking Modes Overview for obtaining more information on display modes.

Void Transaction Utility

With the help of this utility, any Enterprise QuickBooks user or QuickBooks accountant will become capable of removing Bills, Invoices and check transactions simply with a few clicks. It only runs in the Single User Mode. It also does not delete deposits, paychecks, invoices with reimbursable expenses, an online transaction that has already been sent and transactions in a close period. It is located just under the Accountant tab.

Removing and Sending Forms

You need to click on the File and under that you will find Send Forms. The Send Form option shows the amount of time that is needed to send the forms that you have selected to email to your advisors. However, this will not work if you are using QuickBooks email. In case you created the transaction with the sales tax being turned off, making an attempt to remove those transactions from the window of Send Form, after you have turned on the Sales tax will lead to an Unrecoverable Error.

Rebuild Feature or New Verify

From the product information option, you will have the option to review the rebuild and verify status that is present at the right-hand side in the bottom. It is going to take you to screens which will show the errors found and whether the errors have been fixed or not.

Bill Tracker

The Bill Tracker of QuickBooks enables you to view the status of outstanding transactions. You will be able to use some tools of the Bill Tracker for making the managing procedure of the payables efficient and easier.

Connect and Update the Data

Before you are setting QuickBooks for downloading transactions and making all online payments, you might have to contact the financial institution for certain details such as

• Customer ID

• PIN Personal Identification Number or Password

When you are using QuickBooks, you need to use the customer ID and Password/PIN for your Financial Institution Website. In the case of Direct Connect, it might be different. You will have to verify your login information for Direct Connect.

Then you have to follow the steps that have been given below:

• Make a backup of the QuickBooks data file. To get the information to back your data file, you have to select the Help Menu under which you will find QuickBooks. Then you have to search for Backup and then follow the instructions that have been given.

- Download the recent QuickBooks Update. For this, you will have to select QuickBooks Help that you will find under the Help menu. Look for QuickBooks and then choose Updating QuickBooks and then follow the instructions that have been given.

- You will have to shift to the single user mode, in case you want to share a QuickBooks data file among several computers. For obtaining the information, you will have to switch to single user mode and then select QuickBooks Help as before. After this, you will have to search Switch to Single User Mode and after that follow the instructions.

Create an Account for Online Banking

Select the Banking option and then go to Bank Feeds. Under this, you will find the option that says "Set up Bank Feeds for an Account." Your first step will be to find the bank screen and then type the name of your bank in the entry field. When the result shows your bank name, click on it. By the financial institution, after you have clicked your bank name, you will be able to see a screen for selecting the Web Connect to the Direct Connect. You can also be asked to enter the credentials.

In case you have already enrolled in Direct Connect, you have to click Continue. You will see a window that says Connect Financial Institution to QuickBooks. After you have entered the credentials, you have to click on Connect for connecting to your bank account. When you are done with connecting, you will be able to see the accounts that are there in the financial institution which you will be able to use in QuickBooks. When you do not have an account already, you will have to select Create New Account for creating one. If you do intend to download data from a certain account, you have to choose "not add to QuickBooks" that you will find in the drop down menu. Having added the account, you have to click Close.

Setting Up an Account for Online Banking (Web Connect)

You have to log into the website of the financial institution. It is important to download the transaction according to the instructions of the financial intuition. If you have been given the choice for the download format, you have to select QuickBooks Web Connect and then save the particular file to the computer. According to the instructions, you have to save the download to the computer. However, when you open it, your web browser will open QuickBooks and then start importing the transactions. In case you are planning to open the file directly, you should open your Company File in QuickBooks before downloading the transactions.

After this select Banking Menu and you will find Bank Feeds listed under it. Choosing Bank Feeds, you will have to click on Import Web Connect File. You will find an import dialog. Navigate and download the file like previously and then open it. You will find a dialog box with the information about the financial institution. If you already have a suitable account in Chart of Accounts, you have to click on "Use an Existing QuickBooks Account" and after that, enter the name of the account. When done with this, you have to select Continue and then OK for finishing it by confirming.

Matching and Adding Transactions

When you have set up Bank Feeds and then click open the Bank Feeds center, you have to let QuickBooks know the manner in which you have downloaded the transactions. For this, you have to go to the Banking Menu and then open Bank Feeds, where you will find Bank Feeds Center.

Over here you have to select the account that you want to work with and then click on the Transaction List. You will find a colored bar which will indicate,

- Transactions in red that have been changed by rules
- Transactions in orange which need your review
- Transactions in blue which have been automatically matched

Verify or add the QuickBooks in the expense or income account on every transaction.

Updating the Account (Direct Connect) in Bank Feeds (Express Mode)

For this, you have to select Banking menu and then choose Bank Feeds that is listed under it. Then go on to select Bank Feeds center. Choose the account that you want to update in the Bank Feeds window. After having selected the account, you have to click on Download Transaction for starting the update process. When you have multiple accounts in the same bank, you can sync one or all the accounts with the help of the sync button on the upper side at the right-hand corner. When it has been synced the accounts will be updated.

Updating an Account (Web Connect) in Bank Feeds

Select the Banking Menu once and then select Banking Feeds Center by following the previous steps. Choose the account that you want to update in the window of Bank Feeds. When you are done selecting the account, you have to click on the option that says Refresh Account to begin the update process.

When you start the Web Connect download from the financial website, your web browser will give you the option to either open the file or to save it. When you open it, QuickBooks will open and then start off with the import process. When you save it, you will be able to import it later by selecting Banking Menu whereby you will find Bank Feeds and listed under it Import Web Connect File. Then you have to navigate to the Web Connect file that has been located on the computer and then select Open.

This will enable QuickBooks to import the online banking transactions and show you the Transmission Summary. You can review the Online Transmission Summary and then print it just by clicking on Close when the work is done. Following the Web Connect Import, you have to click on the Banking Menu where you will find Bank Feed and under it, Bank Feeds Center. Select the account and then click on the List Transaction button for viewing the downloaded transactions.

Swapping Online Banking Mode

You can conveniently switch from the Express Mode and then to the Classic Mode, which was previously known as the Register Mode. After this, go to the Banking Menu where you find Bank Feeds and listed under it is Change Bank Feeds Mode. You will notice the Company Preferences. In the Bank Feed area, you will find the current mode. You will have to click on the Classic Mode or the Express Mode. Express Mode enables you to change the Rule preferences.

Chapter 10

How To Navigate Through QuickBooks

Here are some answers to the questions that will make navigation easier for you in QuickBooks.

How to Print a Month to Month Profit and Loss Comparison Report.

On the left-hand side of the page, you will find "Reports," click on it and then click on "Profit & Loss." After having selected the transaction date that you desire to view, you have to choose "Customize." Months are listed under Rows/Columns, and you will be able to run the report.

How to Run a Specific Report.

You have to select Report. Above the "Frequently Run" and "Recommended," you will come across a search button for finding any report offered by QuickBooks you require.

How to Find Previous Reconciliation Reports along with Changes.

You need to click on the gear icon which is at the top of the screen. Listed under "Tools," you will find "Reconcile." This will show you your "Reconciliation History" and "Reports." This lists any adjustments or changes that have been made; you will be able to select it through the link for viewing the detail. Choose the statement that you want to print.

Is there Some Other Way to Create Bills, Invoices, Payroll, and Deposits, rather than Selecting the Items Present on the Left Hand Side?

You have to look for a Plus Sign Symbol that is present in the top center of that particular page. After you have selected, you will find a drop down with a list of items to choose from. Here, you will be able to select rapidly at one time anything that you wish to create, print a check, credit memo or just a weekly timesheet.

Where to Go When You Cannot Find a Transaction.

There is a search function with the symbol of a magnifying glass at the top center of the page. You have to select the symbol for entering any amount, check the date and number to find out the transaction. If you want to find something more specific, then you have to opt for "Advanced Search." Then you can choose the transaction type and all that it contains.

Ralph McKinnon

Chapter 11
Advanced Tips And Shortcuts For QuickBooks Users

The aim of QuickBooks is to simplify the bookkeeping and accounting process. That is why it has been developed to be a comprehensive solution for all business accounting tasks. While using the software, you will come across a variety of functions and features designed to reduce the confusion that tends to occur while recording and maintaining transactions and other financial details. Be that as it may, this same comprehensiveness does lead to a new kind of problem. That problem is that some people can find the software to be rather complicated to use, in particular among those who have no prior experience in using these kinds of applications. Even those who know accounting may need to use the software for a considerable period before they get to understand how QuickBooks works.

Intuit has taken steps to bring about ease in the way that you interact with QuickBooks and work with it. This chapter is meant to elucidate some tips and provide you with shortcuts. With their help, you will find it easier to access and use the massive list of features present in QuickBooks. They can help you out in a variety of areas.

Start Using Keyboard Shortcuts

When it comes to using QuickBooks, you can access the various functions required in recording and editing details through the toolbox placed at the top of the window below the menus. However, it can certainly be a chore when working with the software. After all, you will have to keep using the mouse along with the keyboard to access those options and then using them. This is a major problem especially when you have to work with a significant amount of data. Keyboard shortcuts make it easier for you to access a wide variety of functions. After all, you do not have to waste time in moving your hand to and from the mouse every time you wish to access a specific function. Knowing the keyboard shortcuts can also prove to be beneficial as it can help you become faster at using QuickBooks.

Of course, the keyboard shortcuts will be different depending on the operating system that you are using. After all, some keys used by the Mac OS and Microsoft Windows are different. Be that as it may, you shouldn't have to worry. We have provided a list of both the operating systems.

Discovering New Commands

The fact is that the QuickBooks application does not show the keyboard shortcuts for all the commands or the functions besides them in the menus. This does not necessarily mean that there are no corresponding keyboard shortcuts for that particular function or option. Instead, it means that the QuickBooks could not display the shortcut. The easiest way to discover the shortcut is by using the Alt key. In the QuickBooks interface, simply press Alt and you will notice that each item on the Menu Bar now displays an underline beneath one particular letter. For example, the File option will have the F underlined while the View option will have the V underlined. Press the corresponding key to open up that sub-menu. The commands present inside that sub-menu will also have a single letter underlined. Pressing that key will activate that particular command. You can employ this method to access and use all the functions and options available in QuickBooks without having to take your hands away from the keyboard.

List of Shortcuts for Windows

The list of shortcuts given below is meant to be used with the Windows edition of the QuickBooks software. The shortcuts have been organized by the area they are going to be used.

General Shortcuts

- To open QuickBooks without any company file: Control + Double Click
- For suppressing the desktop Windows: Press Alt while opening
- Cancel something: Esc
- Record always: Control + Enter
- For displaying details about QuickBooks: Press F2

Editing Shortcuts

- Edit the transaction which has been selected in the register: Control + E
- Delete the line from the detail area: Control + Del

- Insert a line in the detail area: Control + Insert

Activity Shortcuts

- Display the window of the Charts of Accounts: Control + A
- Display Write Checks: Control + W
- Copy the Transaction in the register: Control + O
- Display Customer: Job list: Control + J
- Delete an item, transaction, invoice or check from the list: Control + D
- Edit the list or the register: Control + E
- Quick Fill and Recall options: Type the first few letters of the name and then press Tab for automatically filling in the rest.
- Go to the register of the transfer account: Control + G
- History of A/P or A/R transactions: Control + H
- Create an Invoice: Control + I
- Display the list for the current field: Control + L
- Memorize the report or the transaction: Control + M
- Display the memorized transaction list: Control + T
- Create a new bill, list item, check or invoice: Control + N
- QuickZoom on the report: Enter
- QuickReport on the list item or transaction: Control + Q

- Display the register: Control + R
- Show the list: Control + S
- Use the list item: Control + U
- Display the transaction journal: Control + Y

Shortcuts for Moving In a Window

- Go to the line above on report or in detail area: Up arrow
- Go to the line below on report or in detail area: Down arrow
- Go to the first item previous month in register or on list: Control + Page Up
- Go to the last item previous month in register or on list: Control + Page Up
- Close the active window: Esc

List of Shortcuts for Mac OS

The shortcuts given below are meant to be used when you are using QuickBooks on a system powered by Mac OS. The list has been divided into categories based on the usage of the shortcuts.

General Shortcuts

- Access the new company command: Option + Command + N
- Access the open company command: Command + O
- Access the close company command: Option + Command + W
- Close the window: Command + N
- Access the Help option in QuickBooks: Command + Question key (?)
- Display the company and product file information: Command + 1

Editing Shortcuts

- Insert a line: Command + Y
- Delete a line: Command + B
- Make an edit: Command + E
- Memorize: Command + Plus Key (+)
- View the transaction history: Command + U
- Go to transfer: Command + G
- Show the list: Command + L
- Use the register: R
- Cancel: Command + Period (.)

Activity Shortcuts

- View the Chart of Accounts: Shift + Command + A
- View Customer: Jobs: Shift + Command + J
- View list of Employees: Shift + Command + E
- View list of Items: Shift + Command + I
- View list of memorized transactions: Shift + Command + M
- View list of Vendors: Shift + Command + V
- Create invoices under Customers: Command + I
- Write checks under banking: Command + K
- View the transaction journal: Command + T

Options for Moving Around In a Window

- Go to the first item on the list or the month's first transaction in register: Command + Page Up
- Go to the last item on the list or the month's first transaction in register: Command + Page Down
- Go to the first transaction in register: Command + Home
- Go to the last transaction in register: Command + End

Common Shortcuts for Both Operating Systems

There are certain shortcuts which are common to both Mac OS and Microsoft Windows. As such, you can use them without any problems in QuickBooks irrespective of the system you are using. The shortcuts have been categorized based on their usage.

Dates Shortcuts

- Next day: Plus Key (+)
- Previous Day: Minus Key (-)
- Today (today starts with T): T
- First day of the week (week starts with W): W
- Last day of the week (week ends with K): K
- First day of the month (month starts with M): M
- Last day of the month (month ends with H): H
- First day of the year (year starts with Y): Y
- Last day of the year (year ends with R): R

Editing Shortcuts

- Increase the check or other numbers by 1: Plus Key (+)
- Decrease the check or other numbers by 1: Minus Key (-)

Shortcuts for Moving In a Window

- Go to the start of the current field: Home key
- Go to the end of the current field: End
- Report column to the left: Left arrow
- Report column to the right: Right arrow
- Go to the next field: Tab
- Go to the previous field: Shift + Tab
- Go to up one screen: Page Up
- Go to down one screen: Page Down

Customize the QuickBooks Icon Bar

The icon bar in QuickBooks is one of the most important sections in the software. It contains a list of all the options that you are going to need the most in your daily operations with the software. Be that as it may, the fact is that there can be certain options which you can access using shortcuts. There can also be options which you need less frequently. On the other hand, there can be options which you need more often and yet they are absent in the icon bar. This could have been a problem certainly. However, Intuit already knows this which is why they have implemented a customization feature.

With the customization feature, you can modify the icon bar so that it can suit your particular needs while working with QuickBooks. This allows you to remove the icons that you do not need while adding those that you are going to use a lot

Removing Icons

Open the View menu in the QuickBooks software. There will be an option called Customize Icon Bar. In the window that opens, you can select the icons that you wish to remove. Once selected, click on the Delete Option to remove them

Adding Icons

To add new icons to the bar, you need to open up the View menu and select the Customize Icon Bar. Click on the Add option. A list of all icons will be displayed. Select the icons that you wish to add to the icon bar. You can even change the label of the icon along with its description. Make the changes that you feel are necessary and then click on the OK option to enable them.

Modifying Icons

As with the other steps, open the Customize Icon Bar option through View menu. A list of the icons currently displayed on the icon bar will be shown. Select the icon you wish to modify. Click the Edit option. You can now make the changes that you want. Once you are satisfied, click OK to save and enable the changes.

Other Changes

There are quite a few other options that you can find inside the Customize Icon Bar window. You can add separators between sets of icons to group them together. You can also modify the order in which the icons will be appearing on the icon bar. You can also choose whether the icons only should be displayed on the icon bar or should their text accompany the icons when being shown.

Start Using the Preferences Option in QuickBooks

One of the most excellent features in QuickBooks is the presence of the setup wizard. This option enables you to complete the basic setup processes required for your company in the application in a very easy manner. You can always choose to complete the setup process on your own. Be that as it may, you will find that the process takes up a long time. Additionally, you will need to put in a lot of effort. By using the setup wizard, these issues are eliminated. What would have taken you an hour or more previously can now be completed in a matter of minutes.

To activate the wizard while setting up a new company in QuickBooks, you should follow the given steps. Open the Edit menu and select the Preferences option. Once the Preferences window has opened, you can set the requisite options of the company by answering the questions asked. Some of the options that you can set are mentioned below.

- Choose between a multi-window and a single-window view.
- Select the default accounts for different activities such as bill payments and writing checks.
- Determine if you want to use purchase orders and inventory.
- Select the default annual interest rate.
- Determine if you wish to make use of multiple currencies.
- Determine if you want to create estimates.

- Select whether you wish to use payroll.
- Mention whether sales tax is charged by you.
- Check whether you track the time.
- Select the reminders that you would prefer.

These are just some of the questions that you need to answer. Based on your answers, QuickBooks will be creating a company file which suits the needs of your business and the work you will be doing with the software. On the other hand, the fact is that the preferences wizard in QuickBooks is not perfect. There will be quite a few things that you will need to setup on your own manually later. Nonetheless, this feature can prove to be useful.

Organize Your Chart of Accounts

If you have used the setup wizard offered by QuickBooks, you will find that a Chart of Accounts has been created for you automatically. The Chart of Accounts will be one of the most important lists as you will be using it every single day. This list is responsible for organizing all the transactions that you will be recording with QuickBooks. This list will contain all the accounts that you need for your bookkeeping and accounting activities such as expenses and incomes along with others. The setup wizard will create a Chart of Accounts that QuickBooks feels is best suited for your business.

On the other hand, the Chart of Accounts created by the setup wizard might not always be suited to your specific needs. You may find that there are more accounts than what you need. Alternatively, you can discover there are not enough accounts to match the needs of the business. As a result, you need to modify the Chart of Accounts and clean it properly so that it can be beneficial for your business.

To edit the Chart of Accounts, click on the Lists menu first. You will find an option called Chart of Accounts which you should click on. You can see the chart that is currently available to you. Right click to start customizing the chart. When you are adding new accounts to the chart, you must make sure that the right account type has been assigned to the new account. After all, it is vital to the accuracy of your accounts and books.

Export Your Reports to Microsoft Office Excel

The reports available in QuickBooks are highly customizable. This is certainly beneficial when you are going to maintain your accounts. However, the features offered by QuickBooks for its reports are nowhere as good as Microsoft Excel, one of the best applications for spreadsheets. With Excel, it becomes possible to manipulate the data for the reports and format them as per requirements. You can even use the data to run hypothetical and what-if scenarios in Excel.

As such, it would be a great advantage to your business if you could use the reports available in QuickBooks with Excel. The good thing is that you can do so thanks to the export option present in QuickBooks. Here is the process you need to follow to make it happen.

- In QuickBooks, open the report which you wish to export to Excel.
- At the top of your report, you will find the Export button. Click on this option.
- You can select the format in which you want to export the report in. There are two options. One of them is the CSV or comma-separated values file, and the other is the Excel workbook format. You can also choose whether the report should be exported as a new Excel workbook or as an existing one.

- You will also find an Advanced Tab in the Export window. Clicking on this tab will give you extra options to preserve some of the formatting features of the QuickBooks report.
- Once you are satisfied, you can click on the Export option to complete the process.

You can now use the exported file with Microsoft Excel.

Tips for Using Advanced Reporting

One of the most interesting features offered by QuickBooks is the Advanced Reporting feature. This feature is rigorously worked upon and developed by Intuit so that it can solve the real reporting needs of the client. It is certainly important to capture the data present in your QuickBooks because of compliance reasons. However, you can use the data to develop reports which can be very helpful in managing your business. This is one of the massive benefits of Advanced Reporting. Be that as it may, there might be a few things about this feature that you didn't know leading to your inability to use it properly. Here are a few tips which can help you make the most of it.

Templates

When you get QuickBooks, you will find a set of templates for Advanced Reporting already available. However, they are not the only templates available. New kinds of report templates have been developed for Advanced Reporting these days. However, you will need to download them separately. Once downloaded, you will then have to import the template into your Advanced Reporting. These templates can provide you with additional starter reports which can suit your specific needs more closely. As a result, your accounting work with QuickBooks is benefited.

Organizing the Report Templates

The report templates for Advanced Reporting are saved separately for every company file you have. For this reason, you will require a method by which you can organize them especially if you have modified or created specific templates for your work. A good method would be to store the reports in a central location.

In order to do so, you should first export the report templates separately. Make sure that you have named each template in a manner that is sensible and easily understandable. Determine an appropriate location and save the template there. The location should allow you to access the templates easily and import the appropriate one when required for another company file. This is extremely important especially when you are working with clients whose needs or industries are similar. It also enables you to import the templates when business management dashboards are created.

Always Use 'Save As' Option

A good tip while working with templates and reports is to use the Save As option instead of the regular "Save" option. After all, it enables you to create multiple files of the same report. You may inadvertently end up making mistakes. An Undo feature is not available to get rid of the errors. By keeping multiple files, you can go back and select the file which does not have the errors. If you do not follow this process, it becomes difficult to edit the report so as to get the error removed.

Think About Your Reports before Entering Large Datasets

It is vital that you do so. You must possess an understanding of the data structure inside QuickBooks. It will be very useful. After all, you have to know that the data is organized so that you can easily look for the data when you are trying to build the reports. It also means that you will have an idea at the very least about the name of the data you are looking for.

After you have considered what data is required, you should enter a few transactions. Then, start creating the reports at the start of the process. For example, you need to think whether you need to use custom fields and list types. The answer to this question can depend on the mixture of reports that is necessary. Since you have entered a sample set of transactions, you can make sure that the result you desire has been achieved in an effective manner.

Take the Help of Intuit

If you are stuck with Advanced Reporting, you can always take the help of Intuit Labs Learning Center. This resource contains some training videos. These videos can help you learn more about Advanced Reporting and how you can use it to your benefit.

Modify QuickBooks to Suit Your Needs Better

Due to the wide range of functions and features available in QuickBooks, using the software can be difficult at times. Be that as it may, you can do it, making it much easier for you to use QuickBooks. At the same time, you can make using it faster. This can be achieved by accessing the Preferences option of the software and customizing it as per your needs and choices.

Accessing the Preferences Option

In order to access the Preferences option, you must click on the Edit menu first. On clicking the Preferences option, a window will open up where a variety of areas is listed on the left column. There will also be two pages for every area, and those pages are Company Preferences and My Preferences. The options listed in My Preferences can be changed by the user logged into QuickBooks, and those changes will only be applicable for that particular user. As for the options listed in the Company Preferences section, they need administration access to be changed. Additionally, these changes will affect all users.

The My Preferences Options for the Desktop View

- Multiple Windows: Enabling this option allows you to keep multiple windows open at any given time.
- Save the Desktop: This option comes into effect when closing QuickBooks. You may have had a few reports when closing QuickBooks. If this option is enabled, you would have to wait for these reports to load when you reopen QuickBooks. You cannot access any option unless those reports load.
- Company File Color Scheme: This option is beneficial when you are working with multiple company files. You can assign a unique color scheme to each company file so that it becomes easier for you to remember which file you are working with.

The My Preferences Options for the General Options

- Pop-Up Messages: You can disable this option to prevent advertisements for other products from QuickBooks from popping up as you use the software.

- Quick Start: On enabling this option, QuickBooks will keep running in the background even after you exit the application. It is in a standby mode for the application. This allows you to load up QuickBooks faster when you need to use it again.

The My Preferences Options for the Checking Options

Default Accounts: With this option, you can set which accounts should be selected by default for paying sales tax, bill payments, writing checks and for making deposits. This will be helpful when you have multiple checking accounts as it can prevent you from entering details into an incorrect account accidentally.

The Company Preferences Options for the Accounting Options

Transaction Warnings: These warnings will be shown when a user is trying to enter a transaction that is older than a specified number of days or over a specified number of days in the future. The dates for each can be specified separately. This feature can prevent errors. This setting becomes enabled for all users.

Set Date and Password: This option allows you to set a password for transactions that take place before the date that you have specified. Any user who tries to enter a transaction before that particular date or modify such a transaction will have to enter the correct password first. This can be a protective measure for preventing the modification of earlier transactions.

Tips for Using Attachments

It is quite possible to upload attachments in QuickBooks and then link them to the appropriate transactions. There are various reasons why you may want to use this feature. Some of the situations in which it can be useful are mentioned as follows.

- Attach the receipts to the expenses or the checks made at other establishments such as stores and restaurants.
- Attach the contracts and graphs to invoices or estimates.
- Attach the bills to the corresponding payments and expense forms.

By using attachments, it is possible to get access to the source documents instantly when you are doing your taxes.

Uploading Attachments

In order to attach something in QuickBooks, the file has to be in a PDF format. While you may be able to get the attachment in PDF from some vendors, in most cases, you will be given them on paper. In such cases, you can take a photo of the bills, contracts or receipts and convert it into PDF. Alternatively, you may want to scan them for the best results. Transfer and store the PDF files in the computer from where you will be uploading them into QuickBooks.

There are four ways by which you can upload the attachments in QuickBooks. They are mentioned below.

- **The Attachments Page**: If you simply want to upload a number of attachments into QuickBooks, then this will the most convenient method. You can link the attachments to specific transactions anytime later.
- **The Bank Feeds Page**: Use this method when you want to upload attachments and link them to different bank transactions as they are being added.
- **Individual Transaction Forms**: It is possible to upload the attachments and get them linked while new transactions are being entered.

- **The Register**: Use this method when you prefer using the register.

Uploading Attachments via the Attachments Page

Of all the four methods mentioned above, you are most likely going to use the attachments page for uploading the files. As such, it will be helpful if you know how you can accomplish this process. Here is a step by step guide.

- Click on the gear icon on the top and then click on Attachments. This will open the Attachments page.
- Once open, you can upload the attachments directly by dragging them and dropping them here.
- Alternatively, you can click on the paper clip icon to browse and select the files you wish to add as attachments.

Once uploaded, there are a variety of functions that you can do with the attachments. You can create an invoice or expense with each attachment. You can also export them to a ZIP file. You can use the batch functions such as editing or printing all of them. You can also easily view the expense or invoice transaction with which each associated attachment.

Remember, that all attachments, once uploaded, will remain stored safely in the cloud. Therefore, you can delete your own copy without any worries. If you wish to get your copy in future, you can use the download option to do so.

You can also sort attachments with the amount property. In order to do, you will have to first edit each attachment and then enter the amount. The amount can be entered as the File Name or in the Notes field.

Uploading Attachments from the Bank Feeds

In order to attach files to the transactions from the bank feeds page, you can use the following guide.

- From the left navigation bar, click on Transactions and then click on Banking.
- In the page, use the add transaction option to create a new transaction.
- While entering the transaction, you will notice an option called Add Attachment.
- Use that option to add the attachment you want for that particular transaction.

Uploading Attachments While Creating New Transactions

The following guide will show you how you can upload attachments while you are creating new transactions.

- Create a new transaction with the Create (+) option.
- On the form of the transaction, scroll down. You will notice the attachments section.
- In this section, you can drag and drop the attachments you want to upload and link.
- If the attachment has already been uploaded, you can click on the Show option to look at the list of attachments that already exist in QuickBooks. Select the ones you wish to link from here.

One excellent feature is that an attachment can be emailed along with the form that it has been linked to. You simply need to choose the option, 'Attach to email' and then click on Save and Send.

Uploading Attachments via the Register

If you are using the register, you can use the following guide for adding attachments.

In the register, turn on the column for the attachments. This can be done through the table gear option.

- Click on the transaction.
- Click on Add attachment to choose and add the file you want.

Pre-Fill Forms in QuickBooks

There are features in QuickBooks that allow you to automate a few tasks. This prevents you from having to manually enter the exact same data multiple times. Pre-fill forms are one of those techniques. With it, you can use fill up forms with content that has been previously entered in another form. It is also called auto-recall setting.

In order to use pre-fill, you will have to turn it on first.

- Click on the gear icon.
- Go to the Company Settings.
- Choose Advanced.
- You will notice the Pre-fill forms option here. Enable it.
- Now that it has been enabled, you can start using the pre-fill feature in your forms. You simply need to enter the details for one particular form. On creating the next form with the same vendor, QuickBooks will

automatically fill in the rest of the details from the previous form. As such, you do not have to enter each detail over and over again. Of course, you can modify any detail in the new form.

There are various types of forms in QuickBooks that are affected by the pre-fill option. They are listed as follows.

- Checks
- Bills
- Delayed credits
- Delayed charges
- Purchase orders
- Expenses
- Credit card credits
- Vendor credits

All of these forms can be accessed through the Create (+) option from the top of the screen in QuickBooks.

When you select a vendor, employee or customer in any of these forms will cause QuickBooks to pre-fill the rest of the transaction. The details will be sourced from the last transaction of the same type that you had saved for that specific person.

It is also possible to use the pre-fill option with timesheets and forms. There is an option called clear all lines located at the bottom of each form. Use this when you need to clear all the details that have been placed thanks to the pre-fill feature.

When Should You Turn On Pre-Fill?

You can certainly enjoy a few conveniences when you turn on the pre-fill option in some situations. Some of them are given below.

Turn pre-fill on when you have to enter expenses or checks on a regular basis to the same vendor who has been assigned to the same expense account. This greatly minimizes the time you spend in writing down the details for each consecutive form. This will still be useful even if the amount tends to change. After all, the other details will remain the same.

It will also be beneficial when your regular expenses and checks have been split into the same but multiple accounts.

When Should You Turn Off Pre-Fill?

In spite of the conveniences provided by pre-fill, there are situations in which you can find this feature to be an annoyance. In such situations, it is better to turn it off. Some of them are mentioned below.

Turn it off when you typically pay vendors for various different things. In other words, if the majority of checks or expenses are associated with the same vendor, but are for different expense accounts then pre-fill will be a problem.

You will also not require this feature if you have few checks or expenses split into multiple accounts.

Another situation where this feature may be a problem is when you share the file in QuickBooks with other users. After all, there may be a risk that one or more of them may forget to modify the amount and record a duplicate transaction accidently instead of a new one.

FAQs on Multi-Factor Authentication

Multi-factor authentication has been implemented by Intuit across all of their products in order to keep your account safe. With it, you can ensure that no one else but you have access to the data of your company.

On implementing this feature, you will be required to use a special one-time confirmation code when you sign in to your account. It is also necessary when you are making changes to your account information like User ID or email.

Now, you may have a number of questions about this feature. The following FAQ should help you out.

Why Must the Account Be Verified When Signing In?

Great care is taken by Intuit and QuickBooks to ensure that the privacy and data of the users. Since your account with QuickBooks can contain confidential information related to your business and its finances, it is vital that it is kept as secure as possible. That is why it is recommended that proper precautions be taken by the users in protecting the information. It is also the reason for the verification procedure.

There are additional steps you can take for ensuring the safety and security of your data in QuickBooks. Most importantly, you should never be using a password that you have used for other products. The security information that you put in should never be basic information or information that can be found online easily. Make sure that you never click on links that appear to be suspicious sent to your email. Instead, you should copy the link and paste it directly into the browser.

Can the verification option be turned off after signing in?

Whenever you sign into your account on a computer or device that you have not used before, QuickBooks will ask you to provide verification for your identity. This is to make sure that the person accessing the data is you. As such, this feature is critical to the security and cannot be turned off.

When you are asked to verify the account, it does not necessarily mean that others have tried accessing your account. Instead, this security feature is considered to be an industry best practice. As a result, it has been implemented in QuickBooks for protecting your data.

What to do when you haven't received the code after checking your email?

You should be patient as it can take some time for the code to be delivered to your email inbox. In some cases, it can take up to several minutes for it to appear.

It is also possible that the email might have sent to your junk or spam folder by mistake. In these cases, you should check these email folders and find out if that is what happened.

If you have not still received the code in spite of several minutes having passed, you can use the "Didn't Receive a Code" option. This option can be found in the window telling you to check your email. Using it will generate a new code. If you do so, you must remember that any code sent to you previously will expire. Therefore, you must always use the confirmation code that is the most recent.

What to do when the code does not work?

Make sure that you have typed the code correctly. If it still does not work, it is possible that you are not using the most recent code having generated several codes. Generate a new code and wait until this code arrives in your email inbox. The process can take a number of minutes. Only use the code that has been sent most recently to you.

Does the code have any expiration time?

Yes. When you generate a code, it is going to be used a single time only, and it will expire once it is used. If you do not use the code, it will expire after 1 hour. The code will also expire if you have requested for a new code. Leaving the browser window will also cause the code to expire.

What are the other options if you cannot wait for the code to be emailed?

If you do not wish to wait for the code to be delivered to you via email, there are a few other options you can try. You must have added your own phone number or that of the office. If you have done so, you can request for the code to be delivered to you by means of an automated phone call or a text message.

This is a recommended option. After all, the code will take a much shorter time span if you have selected the message option. More importantly, you will still be able to verify your identity even if you lose the access to the email account.

What is two-step verification?

Multifactor authentication or two-factor authentication has become a standard in the financial industry. During this process, the user will be required to provide extra verification even after signing in. Typically, a verification code will be sent to the user by means of an automated phone call or a text message.

How to toggle the two-step verification?

In order to have an extra layer of security, it is possible to enable the verification feature any time you sign into QuickBooks with the two-step verification process. You can also use the Google Authenticator App to do so. You can opt out of this feature and deactivate it anytime. Even so, you will still be required to provide verification when you sign in from unrecognized devices.

Ralph McKinnon

Conclusion

Congratulations! You have reached the end of this book. Now that you have done so, you now possess the elementary knowledge to start using QuickBooks for your business. You have also learned some advanced tips and tricks to improve the use of the application further. Go ahead and sync all the appropriate bank accounts so that you can take full advantage of this bookkeeping tool.

You can now start entering all financial details of your business and check the financial condition any time you wish. You can even start generating reports and invoices, all of which can be verified with a few clicks. Start making payments through this application. In short, begin to experience the incredible accounting features of QuickBooks.

This software will help you in viewing the status of your finances, in generating reports that can be verified, creating customized reports, generating invoices, making payments, importing or exporting data from other apps, and creating various lists of customers, vendors, and employees. Now that you know the basics, all you need to keep doing is explore this software. Feel free to make some changes here and there, after all, you are the business owner and you get to decide how you would want to maintain your books of accounts as long as it is in compliance with the required regulatory and legal framework.

Not just this, but because it lets you sync your bank accounts and credit and debit cards as well, you will always stay up-to-date on the position of your finances and be able to create useful budgets. The various steps for troubleshooting and all the new features that come with the updates versions of QuickBooks can be really helpful.

The knowledge you have gained from this book will be more than enough to help you out as you use QuickBooks. Now, you should go ahead and start exploring the software, its features, and options. Feel free to modify the software as per your needs and wishes. After all, it is your very own accounting tool. Just remember to maintain compliance with the appropriate legal and regulatory framework. QuickBooks is a powerful application. With regular use, you can start to apply this application as it was meant to be: a complete accounting and bookkeeping solution.

So, all that is left for you to do is start exploring all the various features of this software in order to discover the ones that work well for you and the ones that don't. You can customize all the options in this software, from the way you want to create the lists to the manner in which you would want to communicate with your client. It really doesn't matter whether or not you are familiar with the accounting concepts and techniques. QuickBooks will do all this for you; you just need to make sure that you are entering the right data. Start exploring to learn more about this software.

I would like to once again thank you for choosing this book. I hope that it proved to be an informative read! All the best!

Ralph McKinnon

CPSIA information can be obtained
at www.ICGtesting.com
Printed in the USA
FSHW022034050219
55507FS